R. L. Trask

The Penguin Guide to Punctuation

PENGUIN BOOKS

PENGUIN BOOKS

Published by the Penguin Group
Penguin Books Ltd, 80 Strand, London WC2R 0RL, England
Penguin Putnam Inc., 375 Hudson Street, New York, New York 10014, USA
Penguin Books Australia Ltd, Ringwood, Victoria, Australia
Penguin Books Canada Ltd, 10 Alcorn Avenue, Toronto, Ontario, Canada M4V 3B2
Penguin Books India (P) Ltd, 11 Community Centre, Panchsheel Park, New Delhi – 110 017, India
Penguin Books (NZ) Ltd, Cnr Rosedale and Airborne Roads, Albany, Auckland, New Zealand
Penguin Books (South Africa) (Pty) Ltd, 24 Sturdee Avenue, Rosebank 2196 South Africa

Penguin Books Ltd, Registered Offices: 80 Strand, London WC2R 0RL, England

www.penguin.com

First published 1997
12

Set in 11½/15½pt Monotype Bembo
Typeset by Rowland Phototypesetting Ltd, Bury St Edmunds, Suffolk
Printed in England by Clays Ltd, St Ives plc

PENGUIN REFERENCE

The Penguin Guide to Punctuation

R. L. Trask was born in western New York State in 1944. For some years he pursued a career in chemistry in the USA and in Turkey. In 1970 he came to England and switched to linguistics, obtaining his Ph.D. from the University of London in 1983. He taught linguistics at the University of Liverpool from 1979 to 1988, since when he has taught in the School of Cognitive and Computing Sciences at the University of Sussex. His special interests are historical linguistics, grammar and the Basque language. He is the author of a number of books, including *A Dictionary of Grammatical Terms in Linguistics*, *Language Change*, *Language: The Basics*, *A Dictionary of Phonetics and Phonology*, *Historical Linguistics*, *The History of Basque*, *The Penguin Dictionary of English Grammar* and *Mind the Gaffe*. He is tired of reading poorly punctuated work, and he hopes this book will help.

Table of Contents

Acknowledgements

I am indebted to Lisa Wale, Max Wheeler, Richard Coates, Margaret Crowther and an anonymous reader for their valuable comments on earlier drafts of this book, and to Lisa Wale for providing many of the examples, and to Donald Wilson for a splendid job of copy-editing. Any remaining shortcomings are my own responsibility.

To the Reader

The book in your hand is a textbook, and it is written for people who find punctuation difficult. If you're not too sure where commas ought to go, if you're puzzled by colons and semicolons, if hyphens and apostrophes are something of a mystery to you, then this book is for you.

The book starts at the beginning and assumes no knowledge of punctuation at all. Each punctuation mark is introduced in turn; its proper use is described with the aid of lots of examples; wherever possible I give you some simple rules for checking your punctuation.

The space devoted to each punctuation mark reflects the degree of difficulty that most people have with it. For example, apostrophes and bracketing commas, which between them probably account for about half of all punctuation mistakes, receive a great deal of discussion, while question marks are dealt with much more briefly, since hardly anybody finds them difficult.

A notable feature of the book is its inclusion of many examples which are badly punctuated. These are always marked with an asterisk (*), and the text explains in each case what is wrong. All of the most frequent punctuation mistakes are treated in this way.

The punctuation described here is the style which is currently the norm in Britain and the Commonwealth. Standard American usage differs in a few respects; in these cases, American usage is also described, but examples of specifically American punctuation are always marked as follows: (A). If you are writing expressly for an American audience, you should follow the American norms.

The book also covers a few topics which are not strictly aspects of punctuation, such as the proper use of capital letters, of contractions and abbreviations and of diacritics. The last chapter goes on to explain the proper way to handle titles, footnotes, references and bibliographies, and it also covers the punctuation of personal and business letters.

Since many people these days do most of their writing at a keyboard, and especially with a word processor, this book also explains the proper use of italics, boldface, small capitals and the special characters available on a word processor.

Chapter 1

Why Learn to Punctuate?

Why should you learn to punctuate properly? After all, many people have made successful careers without ever learning the difference between a colon and a semicolon. Perhaps you consider punctuation to be an inconsequential bit of decoration, not worth spending your valuable time on. Or perhaps you even regard punctuation as a deeply personal matter – a mode of self-expression not unlike your taste in clothes or music.

Well, punctuation is one aspect of written English. How do you feel about other aspects of written English? Would you happily write *pair* when you mean *pear*, because you think the first is a nicer spelling? Would you, in an essay, write *Einstein were a right clever lad, 'e were*, just because that's the way people speak where you come from? Would you consider it acceptable to write *proceed* when you mean *precede*, or vice versa, because you've never understood the difference between them? Probably not – at least, I hope not.

Yet it is quite possible that you do things that are every bit as strange and bewildering when you punctuate your writing. Perhaps you use commas in what we shall soon see are surprising places, merely because you think you might pause there in speech. Perhaps you use semicolons where you should be using colons, because you've never quite understood the difference between them. Or perhaps, if you're really committed to punctuation as self-expression, you just stick in whatever punctuation takes your fancy, because it's *your* piece of work, and so it ought to have *your* punctuation.

The problem with poor punctuation is that it makes life difficult for the reader who needs to read what you've written. That reader shouldn't have to make allowances for your personal tastes in spelling and grammar: she expects to see standard English spellings and standard English grammatical forms. And the same is true for punctuation: she is most unlikely to know what your personal theories of punctuation are, and she won't be interested in them. She'll only be interested in understanding what you've written, and she's going to have trouble understanding it if it's badly punctuated.

When we speak English, we have all sorts of things we can use to make our meaning clear: stress, intonation, rhythm, pauses – even, if all else fails, repeating what we've said. When we write, however, we can't use any of these devices, and the work that they do in speech must be almost entirely handled by punctuation. Consequently, written English has developed a conventional system of punctuation which is consistent and sensible: every punctuation mark has one or more particular jobs to do, and every one should be used always and only to do those jobs. If your reader has to wade through your strange punctuation, she will have trouble following your meaning; at worst, she may be genuinely unable to understand what you've written. If you think I'm exaggerating, consider the following string of words, and try to decide what it's supposed to mean:

> We had one problem only Janet knew we faced bankruptcy

Have you decided? Now consider this string again with differing punctuation:

> We had one problem: only Janet knew we faced bankruptcy.
>
> We had one problem only: Janet knew we faced bankruptcy.
>
> We had one problem only, Janet knew: we faced bankruptcy.
>
> We had one problem only Janet knew we faced: bankruptcy.

Are you satisfied that all four of these have completely different meanings? If so, perhaps you have some inkling of how badly you can confuse your reader by punctuating poorly. What is the reader supposed to make of some feeble effort like this?

> * We had one problem only, Janet knew we faced bankruptcy.

(Remember, an asterisk is used to mark a sentence which is poorly punctuated, or which is otherwise defective.)

Bad punctuation does not require an enormous effort to put right. If you work carefully through this book, then, providing you think carefully about what you're writing as you write it, you will undoubtedly find that your punctuation has improved a great deal. Your readers will thank you for it ever after.

Chapter 2

The Full Stop, the Question Mark and the Exclamation Mark

2.1 The Full Stop

The **full stop** (.), also called the **period**, presents few problems. It is chiefly used to mark the end of a sentence expressing a statement, as in the following examples:

> Terry Pratchett's latest book is not yet out in paperback.
> I asked her whether she could tell me the way to Brighton.
> Chinese, uniquely among the world's languages, is written in a logographic script.
> The British and the Irish drive on the left; all other Europeans drive on the right.

Note how the full stops are used in the following article, extracted from the *Guardian*:

> The opening of Ken Loach's film *Riff-Raff* in New York casts doubt on Winston Churchill's observation that the United States and Britain were two countries separated by a common language. In what must be a first, an entire British film has been given sub-titles to help Americans cut

> through the thick stew of Glaswegian, Geordie, Liverpudlian, West African and West Indian accents. With the arrival of *Riff-Raff*, English as spoken by many British citizens has qualified as a foreign language in the US. Admittedly, the accents on the screen would present a challenge to many people raised on the Queen's English. But it is disconcerting to watch a British film with subtitles, not unlike watching Marlon Brando dubbed into Italian.

There is one common error you must watch out for. Here is an example of it (remember, an asterisk marks a badly punctuated sentence):

> * Norway has applied for EC membership, Sweden is expected to do the same.

Can you see what's wrong with this? Yes, there are two complete statements here, but the first one has been punctuated only with a comma. This is not possible, and something needs to be changed. The simplest way of fixing the example is to change the comma to a full stop:

> Norway has applied for EC membership. Sweden is expected to do the same.

Now each statement has its own full stop. This is correct, but you might consider it clumsy to use two short sentences in a row. If so, you can change the bad example in a different way:

Norway has applied for EC membership, and Sweden is expected to do the same.

This time we have used the connecting word *and* to combine the two short statements into one longer statement, and so now we need only one full stop at the end.

Here are some further examples of this very common error:

★ Bangladesh is one of the world's poorest countries, its annual income is only $80 per person.

★ The British are notoriously bad at learning foreign languages, the Dutch are famously good at it.

★ The proposal to introduce rock music to Radio 3 has caused an outcry, angry letters have been pouring into the BBC.

★ Borg won his fifth straight Wimbledon title in 1980, the following year he lost in the final to McEnroe.

All of these examples suffer from the same problem: a comma has been used to join two complete sentences. In each case, either the comma should be replaced by a full stop, or a suitable connecting word should be added, such as *and* or *while*.

In Chapter 4, I'll explain another way of punctuating these sentences, by using a semicolon.

Full stops are also sometimes used in punctuating abbreviations; this is discussed in Chapter 7.

Summary of full stops

- **Put a full stop at the end of a complete statement.**
- **Do not connect two statements with a comma.**

2.2 The Question Mark

A **question mark** (**?**) is placed at the end of a sentence which is a direct question. Here are some examples:

What is the capital of Wales?
Does anyone have a pen I can borrow?
Who told you that?
In which country did coffee originate?

If the question is a direct quotation, repeating the speaker's exact words, a question mark is still used:

'Have you a pen I can borrow?' she asked.
'How many of you have pets at home?' inquired the teacher.

But a question mark is **not** used in an indirect question, in which the speaker's exact words are not repeated:

She asked if I had a pen she could borrow.
The teacher asked how many of us had pets at home.

Here only a full stop is used, since the whole sentence is now a statement.

The question mark also has one minor use: it may be inserted into the middle of something, inside parentheses, to show that something is uncertain. Here are two examples:

The famous allegorical poem *Piers Plowman* is attributed to William Langland (?1332–?1400).

The Lerga inscription fascinatingly contains the personal name *Vmme Sahar* (?), which looks like perfect Basque.

The question marks on the poet's birth and death dates indicate that those dates are not certain, and the one in the second example indicates that the reading of the name is possibly doubtful.

Summary of question marks

- **Use a question mark at the end of a direct question.**
- **Do not use a question mark at the end of an indirect question.**
- **Use an internal question mark to show that something is uncertain.**

2.3 The Exclamation Mark

The **exclamation mark** (!), known informally as a *bang* or a *shriek*, is used at the end of a sentence or a short phrase which expresses very strong feeling. Here are some examples:

What a lovely view you have here!

That's fantastic!
Johnny, don't touch that!
Help!
Good heavens!
Aaarrgh!

Examples like these are quite normal in those kinds of writing that try to represent ordinary speech – for example, in novels. But exclamation marks are usually out of place in formal writing. Using them frequently will give your work a breathless, almost childish, quality.

An exclamation mark is also usual after an exclamation beginning with *what* or *how*:

What fools people can be!
How well Marshall bowled yesterday!

Note that such sentences are exclamations, and not statements. Compare them with statements:

People can be such fools.
Marshall bowled very well yesterday.

You can also use an exclamation mark to show that a statement is very surprising:

After months of careful work, the scientists finally opened the tomb. It was empty!

It is also permissible to use an exclamation mark to draw attention to an interruption:

On the (rare!) occasion when you use a Latin abbreviation, be sure to punctuate it properly.

Otherwise, you should generally avoid using exclamation marks in your formal writing. Don't write things like this:

★ Do not use exclamation marks in formal writing!
★ In 1848, gold was discovered in California!

Don't use an exclamation mark unless you're certain it's necessary – and **never** use two or three of them in a row:

★ This is a sensational result!!!

This sort of thing is all right in personal letters, but it is completely out of place in formal writing.

Summary of exclamation marks

- **Don't use an exclamation mark unless it's absolutely necessary.**
- **Use an exclamation mark after an exclamation, especially after one beginning with *what* or *how*.**

2.4 A Final Point

Note that a full stop, a question mark or an exclamation mark is **never** preceded by a white space. Things like the following are **wrong**:

★ How well has Darwin's theory stood up ?

A sentence-final punctuation mark is always written next to the last word of the sentence.

2.5 Fragments

A **fragment** is a word or a phrase which stands by itself but which does not make up a complete sentence. Fragments are very common in ordinary speech, in advertisements and even in newspapers. They may be used **very** sparingly in formal writing; when used, they should be followed by a full stop, a question mark or an exclamation mark, as appropriate:

Will the Star Wars project ever be resumed? Probably not.
We need to encourage investment in manufacturing. But how?
Can England beat Australia? Absolutely!

The judicious use of fragments can add vividness to your writing, and they are quite acceptable in writing which is somewhat informal. But don't overdo them: if you use too many fragments, your work will become breathless and disjointed.

Chapter 3
The Comma

The **comma** (,) is very frequently used and very frequently used wrongly. In fact, the rules for using commas are really rather simple, though complicated by the fact that the comma has four distinct uses. To begin with, **forget** anything you've ever been told about using a comma 'wherever you would pause', or anything of the sort; this well-meaning advice is hopelessly misleading. In this book, the four uses of the comma are called the **listing comma**, the **joining comma**, the **gapping comma** and **bracketing commas**. Each use has its own rules, but note that a comma is never preceded by a white space and always followed by a white space.

3.1 The Listing Comma

The **listing comma** is used as a kind of substitute for the word *and*, or sometimes for *or*. It occurs in two slightly different circumstances. First, it is used in a list when three or more words, phrases or even complete sentences are joined by the word *and* or *or*; we might call this construction an *X, Y and Z list*:

The Three Musketeers were Athos, Porthos and Aramis.

Hungarian is spoken in Hungary, in western Rumania, in northern Serbia and in parts of Austria and Slovakia.

You can fly to Bombay via Moscow, via Athens or via Cairo.

Lisa speaks French, Juliet speaks Italian and I speak Spanish.

We spent our evenings chatting in the cafés, watching the sun set over the harbour, stuffing ourselves with the local crabs and getting pleasantly sloshed on retsina.

Note that in all these examples the commas could be replaced by the word *and* or *or*, though the result would be rather clumsy:

The Three Musketeers were Athos and Porthos and Aramis.

Hungarian is spoken in Hungary and in western Rumania and in northern Serbia and in parts of Austria and Slovakia.

You can fly to Bombay via Moscow or via Athens or via Cairo.

Lisa speaks French and Juliet speaks Italian and I speak Spanish.

We spent our evenings chatting in the cafés and watching the sun set over the harbour and stuffing ourselves with the local crabs and getting pleasantly sloshed on retsina.

Observe that you can connect three or more complete sentences with listing commas, as in the Lisa/Juliet example above. Note the difference here:

> Lisa speaks French, Juliet speaks Italian and I speak Spanish.
>
> ★ Lisa speaks French, Juliet speaks Italian.

Remember, you must **not** join two complete sentences with a comma, but three or more complete sentences may be joined with listing commas plus *and* or *or*.

Note also that it is not usual in British usage to put a listing comma before the word *and* or *or* itself (though American usage regularly puts one there). So, in British usage, it is **not** usual to write

> (A) The Three Musketeers were Athos, Porthos, and Aramis.

This is reasonable, since the listing comma is a substitute for the word *and*, not an addition to it. However, you **should** put a comma in this position if doing so would make your meaning clearer:

> My favourite opera composers are Verdi, Puccini, Mozart, and Gilbert and Sullivan.

Here the comma before *and* shows clearly that Gilbert and Sullivan worked together. If you omit the comma, the result might be confusing:

> ★ My favourite opera composers are Verdi, Puccini, Mozart and Gilbert and Sullivan.

Here, the reader might possibly take Mozart and Gilbert as the pair who worked together. The extra comma removes the problem.

A listing comma is also used in a list of modifiers which all modify the same thing. This time there will usually be no *and* present at all, but again such a comma could be replaced by *and* without destroying the sense:

This is a provocative, disturbing book.
Her long, dark, glossy hair fascinated me.

Try replacing the commas by *and*:

This is a provocative and disturbing book.
Her long and dark and glossy hair fascinated me.

The sense is unchanged, though the second example, at least, is much clumsier without the commas.

Observe the difference in the next two examples:

She gave me an antique ivory box.
I prefer Australian red wines to all others.

This time there are no commas. It would be wrong to write

★ She gave me an antique, ivory box.
★ I prefer Australian, red wines to all others.

Why the difference? In these examples, a listing comma cannot be used because there is no list: the word *and* cannot possibly be inserted:

★ She gave me an antique and ivory box.

★ I prefer Australian and red wines to all others.

The reason for the difference is that the modifiers this time do not modify the same thing. In the first example, *ivory* modifies *box*, but *antique* modifies *ivory box*, not just *box*. In the second example, *Australian* modifies *red wines*, not just *wines*.

So the rules are clear:

- **Use a listing comma in a list wherever you could conceivably use the word *and* (or *or*) instead. Do not use a listing comma anywhere else.**
- **Put a listing comma before *and* or *or* only if this is necessary to make your meaning clear.**

3.2 The Joining Comma

The **joining comma** is only slightly different from the listing comma. It is used to join two complete sentences into a single sentence, and it **must** be followed by a suitable connecting word. The connecting words which can be used in this way are *and*, *or*, *but*, *while* and *yet*. Here are some examples:

Norway has applied to join the EC, and Sweden is expected to do the same.

You must hand in your essay by Friday, or you will receive a mark of zero.

Britain has long been isolated in Europe, but now she is beginning to find allies.

Billions of dollars have been hurled into the Star Wars projects, yet we appear to have nothing to show for this colossal expenditure.

A dropped goal counts three points in rugby union, while in rugby league it only counts one point.

Remember, as I pointed out in section 2.1, you **cannot** join two sentences with a comma unless you also use one of these connecting words. All of the following examples are therefore **wrong**:

★ Bangladesh is one of the world's poorest countries, its annual income is only $80 per person.

★ The British are notoriously bad at learning foreign languages, the Dutch are famously good at it.

★ The proposal to introduce rock music to Radio 3 has caused an outcry, angry letters have been pouring into the BBC.

★ Borg won his fifth straight Wimbledon title in 1980, the following year he lost in the final to McEnroe.

Joining two complete sentences with a comma in this way is one of the commonest of all punctuation errors, but one of the easiest to avoid if you pay a little attention to what you're writing. Either you must follow the comma with one of the connecting words listed above, or you must replace the comma with a semicolon, as explained in Chapter 4 below.

Note also that most other connecting words **cannot** be preceded by a joining comma. For example, the connecting words *however*, *therefore*, *hence*, *consequently*, *nevertheless* and *thus* cannot be used after a joining comma. Hence the following examples are also **wrong**:

★ Saturn was long thought to be the only ringed planet, however, this is now known not to be the case.
★ Two members of the expedition were too ill to continue, nevertheless the others decided to press on.
★ Liverpool are five points behind the leaders, therefore they must win both their remaining games.

Sentences like these once again require, not a comma, but a semicolon, as explained in Chapter 4.

The rule is again easy:

- **Use a joining comma to join two complete sentences with one of the words *and, or, but, yet* or *while.* Do not use a joining comma in any other way.**

3.3 The Gapping Comma

The gapping comma is very easy. We use a gapping comma to show that one or more words have been left out when the missing words would simply repeat the words already used earlier in the same sentence. Here is an example:

Some Norwegians wanted to base their national language on the speech of the capital city; others, on the speech of the rural countryside.

The gapping comma here shows that the words *wanted to base their national language*, which might have been repeated, have instead been omitted. This sentence is equivalent to a longer sentence like this:

> Some Norwegians wanted to base their national language on the speech of the capital city; others wanted to base it on the speech of the rural countryside.

Here is another example, which contains both listing commas and gapping commas:

> Italy is famous for her composers and musicians, France, for her chefs and philosophers, and Poland, for her mathematicians and logicians.

(Here I have inserted a listing comma before *and* for the sake of clarity.)

Gapping commas are not always strictly necessary: you can leave them out if the sentence is perfectly clear without them:

> Italy is famous for her composers and musicians, France for her chefs and philosophers, and Poland for her mathematicians and logicians.

Use your judgement: if a sentence seems clear without gapping commas, don't use them; if you have doubts, put them in.

3.4 Bracketing Commas

Bracketing commas (also called **isolating commas**) do a very different job from the other three types. These are the most frequently used type of comma, and they cause more problems than the other types put together. The rule is this: a **pair** of bracketing commas is used to mark off a weak interruption of the sentence – that is, an interruption which does not disturb the smooth flow of the sentence. Note that word 'pair': bracketing commas, in principle at least, always occur in pairs, though sometimes one of them is not written, as explained below. Look carefully at these examples of bracketing commas:

> These findings, we would suggest, cast doubt upon his hypothesis.
>
> Schliemann, of course, did his digging before modern archaeology was invented.
>
> Pratchett has, it would seem, abandoned Rincewind the wizard to the ravages of the Discworld.
>
> Darwin's *Origin of Species*, published in 1859, revolutionized biological thinking.
>
> The Pakistanis, like the Australians before them, have exposed the shortcomings of the England batting order.
>
> Rupert Brooke, who was killed in the war at the age of twenty-eight, was one of our finest poets.
>
> We have been forced to conclude, after careful study of

> the data, that the proposed correlations, in spite of their obvious appeal, do not stand up.

In each case a weak interruption has been set off by a pair of bracketing commas. (The last example has two weak interruptions.) Now notice something important: in every one of these examples, the weak interruption set off by bracketing commas could, in principle, be removed from the sentence, and the result would still be a complete sentence that made good sense. Try this with some of the examples:

> These findings cast doubt upon his hypothesis.
> Pratchett has abandoned Rincewind the wizard to the ravages of the Discworld.
> The Pakistanis have exposed the shortcomings of the England batting order.
> We have been forced to conclude that the proposed correlations do not stand up.

This is **always** the case with bracketing commas, and it gives you a simple way of checking your punctuation. If you have set off some words with a pair of bracketing commas, and you find you can't remove those words without destroying the sentence, you have done something wrong. Here is an example of wrong use, taken from Carey (1958):

> ★ Yet, outside that door, lay a whole new world.

If you try to remove the words *outside that door*, the result is ★ *Yet lay a whole new world*, which is not a sentence. The problem here is that *outside that door* is not an interruption at all: it's an essential part of the sentence. So, the bracketing commas shouldn't be there. Just get rid of them:

Yet outside that door lay a whole new world.

Here is another example:

★ She groped for her cigarettes, and finding them, hastily lit one.

This time, if you try to remove the words *and finding them*, the result is ★ *She groped for her cigarettes hastily lit one*, which is again not a sentence. The problem is that the interruption in this sentence is only the sequence *finding them*; the word *and* is not part of the interruption, but an essential part of the sentence. So move the first comma:

She groped for her cigarettes and, finding them, hastily lit one.

Now check that the interruption has been correctly marked off:

She groped for her cigarettes and hastily lit one.

This is a good sentence, so you have now got the bracketing commas in the right places.

Since bracketing commas really do confuse many people, let's look at some further examples:

★ Stanley was a determined, even ruthless figure.

What's wrong here? Well, that comma can't possibly be a listing comma, a joining comma or a gapping comma; therefore it must be intended as a bracketing comma. But where is the interruption it is trying to bracket? It can't be the three words at the end: ★ *Stanley was a determined* is so much gibberish. In fact, the weak interruption here is the phrase *even ruthless*, and the bracketing commas should show this:

> Stanley was a determined, even ruthless, figure.

This is perfect, since now the bracketed interruption can be safely removed:

> Stanley was a determined figure.

Sometimes this very common type of mistake will not disturb your reader too much, but on occasion it can be utterly bewildering:

> ★ The Third Partition of Poland was the last, and undoubtedly the most humiliating act in the sorry decline of the once-powerful kingdom.

Here the sequence before the comma, *The Third Partition of Poland was the last*, seems to make sense by itself, but unfortunately not the sense that the writer intends. With only one comma, the reader will surely assume the writer means 'The Third Partition of Poland was the last [partition of Poland]', will go on to assume that the word *undoubtedly* begins another statement, and will be left floundering when she abruptly comes to a full stop instead of a verb. The essential second bracketing comma removes the problem:

> The Third Partition of Poland was the last, and undoubtedly the most humiliating, act in the sorry decline of the once-powerful kingdom.

Here is another example of a type which often causes trouble:

> The people of Cornwall, who depend upon fishing for their livelihood, are up in arms over the new EC quotas.

As always, we could in principle remove the bracketed interruption to produce a sensible sentence:

> The people of Cornwall are up in arms over the new EC quotas.

But note carefully: this sentence is talking about *all* the people of Cornwall, and not just some of them, and hence so was the original sentence. The weak interruption in the original sentence is merely adding some extra information about the people of Cornwall. Now consider this different example:

> The people of Cornwall who depend upon fishing for their livelihood are up in arms over the new EC quotas.

This time there are no bracketing commas because there is no interruption: now we are not talking about *all* the people of Cornwall, but only about *some* of them: specifically, about the ones who depend upon fishing for their livelihood. Here the phrase *who depend upon fishing for their livelihood* is not an interruption but an essential part of the sentence, and hence it receives no bracketing commas.

The difference illustrated by the last two examples is the difference between what are called *restrictive* (or *defining*) *relative clauses* and *non-restrictive* (or *non-defining*) *relative clauses*. A restrictive clause is required to identify what is being talked about, and it never receives bracketing commas. A non-restrictive clause is not required for identification, but only adds further information, and it always receives bracketing commas. Here are some further examples of the difference. First, some non-restrictive clauses:

> Margaret Thatcher, who hated trains, refused to consider privatizing the railways.
>
> The rings of Saturn, which can be easily seen with a small telescope, are composed of billions of tiny particles of rock.
>
> Bertrand Russell struck up a surprising friendship with D. H. Lawrence, whose strange ideas seemed to fascinate him.
>
> Noam Chomsky is the originator of the innateness hypothesis, according to which we are born already knowing what human languages are like.

Observe that, in each case, the non-restrictive clause bracketed by commas could be removed without destroying the sense. Each of these clauses merely adds more information about Margaret Thatcher, the rings of Saturn, D.H. Lawrence and the innateness hypothesis, and this extra information is not required to let the reader know who or what is being talked about.

The next few examples illustrate restrictive clauses:

The pictures which are being sent back by the Hubble Space Telescope may revolutionize our understanding of the universe.

The Russian scholar Yuri Knorosov has provided an interpretation of the Mayan inscriptions which is now generally accepted.

Because of problems with the test, all the people who were told they were HIV-negative are being recalled.

Anybody who still believes that Uri Geller has strange powers should read James Randi's book.

Here, without the restrictive clauses, the reader would not know which pictures, which interpretation or which people are being talked about, and that *anybody* in the last example would make no sense at all, and so there are no bracketing commas.

Observe that a proper name always uniquely identifies the person or thing being talked about, and hence a proper name never receives a restrictive clause (with no commas) in normal circumstances:

★ I discussed this with Johanna Nichols who is a specialist in Caucasian languages.

Here the clause following the proper name *Johanna Nichols* must be set off by a bracketing comma. The only exception is the special case in which a proper name is preceded by *the* to indicate that we are talking about some particular stage in time:

> The Napoleon who retreated from Moscow was a sadder and wiser man than the Napoleon who had previously known only unbroken triumph.

Finally, note that the word *that* can *only* introduce a restrictive clause, and so a relative clause with *that* can never take bracketing commas:

> * The European powers, that were busily carving up Africa, paid no attention to the boundaries between rival ethnic groups.

If this relative clause is intended to identify the European powers under discussion, then the commas should be removed; if, however, the sentence is meant to be about the European powers generally, the commas are correct but the *that* must be changed to *which*.

Sometimes a weak interruption comes at the beginning or at the end of its sentence. In such a case, one of the two bracketing commas would logically fall at the beginning or the end of the sentence – but we **never** write a comma at the beginning or at the end of a sentence. As a result, only one of the two bracketing commas is written in this case:

> All in all, I think we can say that we've done well.

I think we can say that we've done well, all in all.

When the weak interruption *all in all* comes at the beginning of the sentence, it has only a following comma; when it comes at the end, it has only a preceding comma. Compare what happens when the interruption comes in the middle:

I think we can say that, all in all, we've done well.

Now the interruption has two bracketing commas. Regardless of where the interruption is placed, it could be removed to give the perfectly good sentence *I think we can say that we've done well.*

Here are some further examples of weak interruptions that come at the beginning or at the end.

At the beginning:

Having worked for years in Italy, Susan speaks excellent Italian.
Unlike most nations, Britain has no written constitution.
Although Mercury is closer to the sun, Venus has the higher surface temperature.
After capturing the Aztec capital, Cortés turned his attention to the Pacific.

And at the end:

The use of dictionaries is not allowed, which strikes me as preposterous.
The pronunciation of English is changing rapidly, we are told.

The Rose Parade is held in Pasadena, a suburb of Los Angeles.

Once again, the words set off by a single bracketing comma in these examples could be removed to leave a good sentence. Check this for yourself.

There are a number of common words which typically introduce weak interruptions containing complete sentences. Among the commonest of these are *although*, *though*, *even though*, *because*, *since*, *after*, *before*, *if*, *when* and *whenever*. Weak interruptions introduced by these words are usually rather long, and therefore they most often come at the beginning or at the end of a sentence. Some examples:

Although Australian wines are a fairly new phenomenon, they have already established a formidable reputation.

After the Roman legions withdrew from Britain, the British found themselves defenceless against Irish and Viking raids.

If there are any further cuts in funding, our library will be severely affected.

Hitler could never have invaded Britain successfully, because their excellent rail system would have allowed the British to mass defenders quickly at any beachhead.

Columbus is usually credited with discovering America, even though the Vikings had preceded him by several centuries.

There is just one case in which you might find yourself apparently following all the rules but still using bracketing commas wrongly. Consider the following example, and try to decide if the comma is properly used:

> Note that in each of these examples, the material set off by commas could be removed without destroying the sentence.

The comma in this example is clearly not a listing comma, a joining comma or a gapping comma. Is it a bracketing comma? Try removing the words before the comma:

> The material set off by commas could be removed without destroying the sentence.

This appears to be a good sentence, and so you might think that the original example was correctly punctuated. But it is not. The problem is that the original sentence was an instruction to notice something, and the words *Note that* are therefore an essential part of the sentence, not part of the interruption. The interruption, quite clearly, consists only of the words *in each of these examples*. When we tried to remove the first seven words, we got something that was a sentence, purely by accident, but a sentence in which the original meaning had been partly destroyed. The original attempt at punctuating was therefore wrong, and it must be corrected by adding the second bracketing comma around the interruption:

Note that, in each of these examples, the material set off by commas could be removed without destroying the sentence.

Now the interruption marked off by the bracketing commas can be safely removed without wrecking the sense of the sentence:

Note that the material set off by commas could be removed without destroying the sentence.

Therefore, when you are checking your bracketing commas, make sure that the words enclosed in commas really do make up an interruption, and do not include an essential part of the sentence.

In many cases a weak interruption does not absolutely require bracketing commas. Thus either of the following is fine:

Shortly before the war, he was living in Paris.
Shortly before the war he was living in Paris.

With or without the bracketing comma, this sentence is perfectly clear. Sometimes, however, the bracketing comma is absolutely essential to avoid misleading the reader:

*Just before unloading the trucks were fired upon.

Here the reader naturally takes *Just before unloading the trucks* as a single phrase, and is left floundering as a result. A bracketing comma removes the difficulty:

Just before unloading, the trucks were fired upon.

The best way to avoid problems of this sort is, of course, to read what you've written. Remember, it is **your** job to make your meaning clear to the reader. The reader should not have to struggle to make sense of what you've written.

Here are the rules for using bracketing commas:

- **Use a PAIR of bracketing commas to set off a weak interruption which could be removed from the sentence without destroying it.**
- **If the interruption comes at the beginning or the end of the sentence, use only one bracketing comma.**
- **Make sure the words set off are really an interruption.**

3.5 Summary of Commas

There are four types of comma: the **listing comma**, the **joining comma**, the **gapping comma** and **bracketing commas**.

A listing comma can always be replaced by the word *and* or *or*:

Vanessa seems to live on eggs, pasta and aubergines.
Vanessa seems to live on eggs and pasta and aubergines.

Choose an article from the *Guardian*, the *Independent* or *The Times*.
Choose an article from the *Guardian* or the *Independent* or *The Times*.

Stanley was an energetic, determined and even ruthless figure.
Stanley was an energetic and determined and even ruthless figure.

A joining comma must be followed by one of the connecting words *and*, *or*, *but*, *yet* or *while*:

The report was due last week, but it hasn't appeared yet.
The motorways in France and Spain are toll roads, while those in Britain are free.

A gapping comma indicates that you have decided not to repeat some words which have already occurred in the sentence:

Jupiter is the largest planet and Pluto, the smallest.

Bracketing commas always come in pairs, unless one of them would come at the beginning or the end of the sentence, and they always set off a weak interruption which could in principle be removed from the sentence:

My father, who hated cricket, always refused to watch me play.
We have a slight problem, to put it mildly.

If you're not sure about your commas, you can check them by using these rules. Ask yourself these questions:

1. Can the comma be replaced by *and* or *or*?
2. Is it followed by one of the connecting words *and*, *or*, *but*, *yet* or *while*?

3. Does it represent the absence of repetition?
4. Does it form one of a pair of commas setting off an interruption which could be removed from the sentence?

If the answer to all these questions is 'no', you have done something wrong. Try these questions on the following example:

> The publication of *The Hobbit* in 1937, marked the beginning of Tolkien's career as a fantasy writer.

Can that comma be replaced by *and* or *or*? No – the result would make no sense. Is it followed by a suitable connecting word? No – obviously not. Have some repeated words been left out? No – certainly not. Is it one of a pair? Not obviously, but maybe the interruption comes at the beginning or the end. Can the words before the comma be safely removed? No – what's left is not a sentence. Can the words after the comma be removed? No – the result would still not be a sentence.

We get the answer 'no' in every case, and therefore that comma shouldn't be there. Get rid of it:

> The publication of *The Hobbit* in 1937 marked the beginning of Tolkien's career as a fantasy writer.

Try another example:

> Josie originally wanted to be a teacher, but after finishing university, she decided to become a lawyer instead.

Let's check the first comma. Can it be replaced by *and* or *or*? Certainly not. Is it followed by a suitable connecting word? Yes, it's followed by *but*. So the first comma looks okay at the moment. Now the second comma. Can it be replaced? No. Is it followed by a connecting word? No. Does it stand for a repetition? No. Is it one of a pair? Possibly – but can we remove the words set off by the pair of commas? Let's try:

> Josie originally wanted to be a teacher she decided to become a lawyer instead.

This is clearly wrong. Is there an interruption at the end of the sentence?

> Josie originally wanted to be a teacher, but after finishing university.

This is even worse. (It does make sense of a sort, but the wrong sense.) There's something wrong with that second comma. Try getting rid of it:

> Josie originally wanted to be a teacher, but after finishing university she decided to become a lawyer instead.

This makes perfect sense, and it obeys all the rules. The comma after *teacher* is a joining comma, but that second comma was a mistake.

In fact, there's another way of fixing this sentence. The words *after finishing university* actually make up a weak interruption. So you can, if you prefer, put a pair of bracketing commas around these words:

Josie originally wanted to be a teacher, but, after finishing university, she decided to become a lawyer instead.

Check that this new version is also correct by removing the words set off by the pair of bracketing commas:

Josie originally wanted to be a teacher, but she decided to become a lawyer instead.

This is a good sentence, so the version with three commas is also correct. Remember, you don't **have** to set off a weak interruption with bracketing commas, as long as the meaning is clear without them, but, if you do use bracketing commas, make sure you use both of them.

In sum, then:

- **Use a listing comma in a list where *and* or *or* would be possible instead.**
- **Use a joining comma before *and, or, but, yet* or *while* followed by a complete sentence.**
- **Use a gapping comma to show that words have been omitted instead of repeated.**
- **Use a pair of bracketing commas to set off a weak interruption.**

Finally, the use of commas in writing numbers is explained in section 9.8.

Chapter 4
The Colon and the Semicolon

4.1 The Colon

The **colon** (:) seems to bewilder many people, though it's really rather easy to use correctly, since it has only one major use. But first please note the following: the colon is **never** preceded by a white space; it is **always** followed by a single white space in normal use, and it is **never**, **never**, **never** followed by a hyphen or a dash – in spite of what you might have been taught in school. One of the commonest of all punctuation mistakes is following a colon with a completely pointless hyphen.

The colon is used to indicate that what follows it is an explanation or elaboration of what precedes it. That is, having introduced some topic in more general terms, you can use a colon and go on to explain that same topic in more specific terms. Schematically:

More general: more specific.

A colon is nearly always preceded by a complete sentence; what follows the colon may or may not be a complete sentence, and it may be a mere list or even a single word. A colon is not normally followed by a capital letter in British usage, though American usage often prefers to use a capital. Here are some examples:

Africa is facing a terrifying problem: perpetual drought.
[Explains what the problem is.]
The situation is clear: if you have unprotected sex with a stranger, you risk AIDS.
[Explains what the clear situation is.]
She was sure of one thing: she was not going to be a housewife.
[Identifies the one thing she was sure of.]
Mae West had one golden rule for handling men: 'Tell the pretty ones they're smart and tell the smart ones they're pretty.'
[Explicates the golden rule.]
Several friends have provided me with inspiration: Tim, Ian and, above all, Larry.
[Identifies the friends in question.]
We found the place easily: your directions were perfect.
[Explains why we found it easily.]
I propose the creation of a new post: School Executive Officer.
[Identifies the post in question.]

Very occasionally, the colon construction is turned round, with the specifics coming first and the general summary afterwards:

Saussure, Sapir, Bloomfield, Chomsky: all these have revolutionized linguistics in one way or another.

Like all inverted constructions, this one should be used sparingly.

While you're studying these examples, notice again that the colon is never preceded by a white space and never followed by anything except a single white space.

You should **not** use a colon, or any other mark, at the end of a heading which introduces a new section of a document: look at the chapter headings and section headings in this book. It is, however, usual to use a colon after a word, phrase or sentence in the middle of a text which introduces some following material which is set off in the middle of the page. There are three consecutive examples of this just above, in the second, third and fourth paragraphs of this section.

The colon has a few minor uses. First, when you cite the name of a book which has both a title and a subtitle, you should separate the two with a colon:

I recommend Chinnery's book *Oak Furniture: The British Tradition*.

You should do this even though no colon may appear on the cover or the title page of the book itself.

Second, the colon is used in citing passages from the Bible:

The story of Menahem is found in II Kings 15:14–22.

Third, the colon may be used in writing ratios:

> Among students of French, women outnumber men by more than 4:1.

In formal writing, however, it is usually preferable to write out ratios in words:

> Among students of French, women outnumber men by more than four to one.

Fourth, in American usage, a colon is used to separate the hours from the minutes in giving a time of day: *2:10*, *11:30* (A). British English uses a full stop for this purpose: *2.10*, *11.30*.

Observe that, exceptionally, the colon is **not** followed by a white space in these last three situations.

Finally, see Chapter 10 for the use of the colon in formal letters and in citing references to published work.

4.2 The Semicolon

The **semicolon** (;) has only one major use. It is used to join two **complete** sentences into a single written sentence when all of the following conditions are met:

1. The two sentences are felt to be too closely related to be separated by a full stop;
2. There is no connecting word which would require a comma, such as *and* or *but*;
3. The special conditions requiring a colon are absent.

Here is a famous example:

It was the best of times; it was the worst of times.

A semicolon can always, in principle, be replaced either by a full stop (yielding two separate sentences) or by the word *and* (possibly preceded by a joining comma). Thus Dickens might have written:

It was the best of times. It was the worst of times. **or**
It was the best of times, and it was the worst of times.

The use of the semicolon suggests that the writer sees the two smaller sentences as being more closely related than the average two consecutive sentences; preferring the semicolon to *and* often gives a more vivid sense of the relation between the two. But observe carefully: the semicolon **must** be both preceded by a complete sentence and followed by a complete sentence. Do **not** use the semicolon otherwise:

★ I don't like him; not at all.
★ In 1991 the music world was shaken by a tragic event; the death of Freddy Mercury.
★ We've had streams of books on chaos theory; no fewer than twelve since 1988.
★ After a long and bitter struggle; Derrida was awarded an honorary degree by Cambridge University.

These are all **wrong**, since the semicolon does not separate complete sentences. (The first and last of these should have only a bracketing comma, while the second and third meet the requirements for a colon and should have one.) Here are some further examples of correct use:

> Tolkien published *The Hobbit* in 1937; the first volume of *The Lord of the Rings* followed in 1954.
>
> The Cabernet Sauvignon grape predominates in the Bordeaux region; Pinot Noir holds sway in Burgundy; Syrah is largely confined to the Rhône valley.
>
> Women's conversation is cooperative; men's is competitive.

If a suitable connecting word is used, then a joining comma is required, rather than a semicolon:

> Women's conversation is cooperative, while men's is competitive.

A semicolon would be impossible in the last example, since the sequence after the comma is not a complete sentence.

Note, however, that certain connecting words **do** require a preceding semicolon. Chief among these are *however*, *therefore*, *hence*, *thus*, *consequently*, *nevertheless* and *meanwhile*:

> Saturn was long thought to be the only ringed planet; however, this is now known not to be the case.
>
> The two warring sides have refused to withdraw from the airport; consequently aid flights have had to be suspended.

Observe that in these examples the sequence after the semicolon **does** constitute a complete sentence. And note particularly that the word *however* must be separated by a semicolon (or a full stop) from a preceding complete sentence; this is a very common mistake.

There is one special circumstance in which a semicolon may be used to separate sequences which are not complete sentences. This occurs when a sentence has become so long and so full of commas that the reader can hardly be expected to follow it without some special marking. In this case, we sometimes find semicolons used instead of commas to mark the most important breaks in the sentence: such semicolons are effectively being used to mark places where the reader can pause to catch her breath. Consider the following example:

> In Somalia, where the civil war still rages, western aid workers, in spite of frantic efforts, are unable to operate, and the people, starving, terrified and desperate, are flooding into neighbouring Ethiopia.

This sentence is perfectly punctuated, but the number of commas is somewhat alarming. In such a case, the comma marking the major break in the sentence may be replaced by a semicolon:

> In Somalia, where the civil war still rages, western aid workers, in spite of frantic efforts, are unable to operate; and the people, starving, terrified and desperate, are flooding into neighbouring Ethiopia.

Such use of the semicolon as a kind of 'super-comma' is not very appealing, and you should do your best to avoid it. If you find one of your sentences becoming dangerously long and full of commas, it is usually better to start over and rewrite it, perhaps as two separate sentences:

> In Somalia, where the civil war still rages, western aid workers, in spite of frantic efforts, are unable to operate. Meanwhile the people, starving, terrified and desperate, are flooding into neighbouring Ethiopia.

In any case, don't get into the habit of using a semicolon (or anything else) merely to mark a breathing space. Your reader will be perfectly capable of doing his own breathing, providing your sentence is well punctuated; punctuation is an aid to understanding, not to respiration.

4.3 The Colon and the Semicolon Compared

Since the use of the colon and the semicolon, although simple in principle, presents so many difficulties to uncertain punctuators, it will be helpful to contrast them here. Consider first the following two sentences:

> Lisa is upset. Gus is having a nervous breakdown.

The use of two separate sentences suggests that there is no particular connection between these two facts: they just happen to be true at the same time. No particular inference can be drawn, except perhaps that things are generally bad. Now see what happens when a semicolon is used:

Lisa is upset; Gus is having a nervous breakdown.

The semicolon now suggests that the two statements are related in some way. The likeliest inference is that the cause of Lisa's annoyance and the cause of Gus's nervous breakdown are the same. Perhaps, for example, both are being disturbed by building noise next door. (Remember, a semicolon connects two sentences which are related.) Now try it with a colon:

Lisa is upset: Gus is having a nervous breakdown.

This time the colon shows explicitly that Gus's nervous breakdown is the reason for Lisa's distress: Lisa is upset **because** Gus is having a nervous breakdown. (Remember, a colon introduces an explanation or elaboration of what has come before.)

Consider another example:

I have the answer. Mike's solution doesn't work.

Here we have two independent statements: my answer and Mike's solution may possibly have been directed at the same problem, but nothing implies this, and equally they may have been directed at two entirely distinct problems. Now, with a semicolon:

I have the answer; Mike's solution doesn't work.

The semicolon shows that the two statements are related, and strongly implies that Mike and I were working on the same problem. Finally, with a colon:

I have the answer: Mike's solution doesn't work.

This time the use of the colon indicates that the failure of Mike's solution is exactly the answer which I have obtained: that is, what I have discovered is that Mike's solution doesn't work.

If you understand these examples, you should be well on your way to using colons and semicolons correctly.

Summary of colons and semicolons

- **Use a colon to separate a general statement from following specifics.**
- **Use a semicolon to connect two complete sentences not joined by *and, or, but, yet* or *while*.**

Chapter 5
The Apostrophe

The **apostrophe** (') is the most troublesome punctuation mark in English, and perhaps also the least useful. No other punctuation mark causes so much bewilderment, or is so often misused. On the one hand, shops offer ★ *pizza's*, ★ *video's*, ★ *greeting's cards* and ★ *ladie's clothing*; on the other, they offer ★ *childrens shoes* and ★ *artists supplies*. The confusion about apostrophes is so great, in comparison with the small amount of useful work they perform, that many distinguished writers and linguists have argued that the best way of eliminating the confusion would be to get rid of this troublesome squiggle altogether and never use it at all.

They are probably right, but unfortunately the apostrophe has not been abolished yet, and it is a blunt fact that the incorrect use of apostrophes will make your writing look illiterate more quickly than almost any other kind of mistake. I'm afraid, therefore, that, if you find apostrophes difficult, you will just have to grit your teeth and get down to work.

5.1 Contractions

The apostrophe is used in writing **contractions** – that is, shortened forms of words from which one or more letters have been omitted. In standard English, this generally happens only with a small number of conventional items, mostly involving verbs. Here are some of the commonest examples, with their uncontracted equivalents:

it's	it is *or* it has
we'll	we will *or* we shall
they've	they have
can't	can not
he'd	he would *or* he had
aren't	are not
she'd've	she would have
won't	will not

Note in each case that the apostrophe appears precisely in the position of the omitted letters: we write *can't*, not ★ *ca'nt*, and *aren't*, not ★ *are'nt*. Note also that the irregular contraction *won't* takes its apostrophe between the *n* and the *t*, just like all other contractions involving *not*. And note also that *she'd've* has two apostrophes, because material has been omitted from two positions.

It is not wrong to use such contractions in formal writing, but you should use them sparingly, since they tend to make your writing appear less than fully formal. Since I'm trying to make this book seem chatty rather than intimidating, I've been using a few contractions here and there, though not as many as I might have used. But I advise you **not** to use the more colloquial contractions like *she'd've* in your formal writing: these things, while perfectly normal in speech, are a little too informal for careful writing.

Such contractions represent the most useful job the apostrophe does for us, since, without it, we would have no way of expressing in writing the difference between *she'll* and *shell*, *he'll* and *hell*, *can't* and *cant*, *I'll* and *ill*, *we're* and *were*, *she'd* and *shed*, *we'll* and *well*, and perhaps a few others.

A few words which were contractions long ago are still conventionally written with apostrophes, even though the longer forms have more or less dropped out of use. There are so few of these that you can easily learn them all. Here are the commonest ones, with their original longer forms:

o'clock	of the clock
Hallowe'en	Halloweven
fo'c's'le	forecastle
cat-o'-nine-tails	cat-of-nine-tails
ne'er-do-well	never-do-well
will-o'-the-wisp	will-of-the-wisp

Some generations ago there were rather more contractions in regular use in English; these other contractions are now archaic, and you wouldn't normally use any of them except in direct quotations from older written work. Here are a few of them, with their longer forms:

'tis	it is
'twas	it was
o'er	over
e'en	even

There are other contractions which are often heard in speech. Here are a few:

'Fraid so.	'Nother drink?
I s'pose so.	'S not funny.

It is, of course, never appropriate to use such colloquial forms in formal writing, except when you are explicitly writing about colloquial English. If you do have occasion to cite or use these things, you should use apostrophes in the normal way to mark the elided material.

In contemporary usage, there are a few unusual phrases in which the word *and* is written as *'n'*, with two apostrophes (**not** quotation marks); the commonest of these is *rock 'n' roll*, which is always so written, even in formal writing. One or two more of these are perhaps acceptable in formal writing, such as *pick 'n' mix* and possibly *surf 'n' turf* (this last is a cute label for a particular type of food). But don't overdo it: write *fish and chips*, even though you may see *fish 'n' chips* on takeaway shop signs or even on restaurant menus.

Contractions must be carefully distinguished from **clipped forms**. A clipped form is a full word which happens to be derived by chopping a piece off a longer word, usually one with the same meaning. Clipped forms are very common in English; here are a few, with their related longer forms:

gym	gymnasium
ad	advertisement
pro	professional
deli	delicatessen
hippo	hippopotamus
bra	brassière
tec	detective
flu	influenza
phone	telephone
copter	helicopter
cello	violoncello
gator	alligator
quake	earthquake

Such clipped forms are **not** regarded as contractions, and they should not be written with apostrophes. Writing things like *hippo'*, *bra'*, *'cello* and *'phone* will, not to mince words, make you look like an affected old fuddy-duddy who doesn't quite approve of anything that's happened since 1912. Of course, some of these clipped forms are still rather colloquial, and in formal writing you would normally prefer to write *detective* and *alligator*, rather than *tec* and *gator*. Others, however, are perfectly normal in formal writing: even the most dignified music critic would call Ofra Harnoy's instrument a *cello*; he would no more use *violoncello* than he would apply the word *omnibus* to a London double-decker.

Important note: Contractions must also be carefully distinguished from *abbreviations*. Abbreviations are things like *Mr* for *Mister*, *lb.* for *pound(s)*, BC for *before Christ* and *e.g.* for *for example*. Their use is explained in section 7.2.

Finally, there are a few circumstances in which apostrophes are used to represent the omission of some material in cases which are not exactly contractions. First, certain surnames of non-English origin are written with apostrophes: *O'Leary* (Irish), *d'Abbadie* (French), *D'Angelo* (Italian), *M'Tavish* (Scots Gaelic). These are not really contractions because there is no alternative way of writing them.

Second, apostrophes are sometimes used in representing words in non-standard forms of English: thus the Scots poet Robert Burns writes *gi'* for *give* and *a'* for *all*. You are hardly likely to need this device except when you are quoting from such work.

Third, a year is occasionally written in an abbreviated form with an apostrophe: *Pío Baroja was a distinctive member of the generation of '98*. This is only normal in certain set expressions; in my example, the phrase *generation of '98* is an accepted label for a certain group of Spanish writers, and it would not be normal to write ★ *generation of 1898*. Except for such conventional phrases, however, you should always write out years in full when you are writing formally: do **not** write something like ★ *the '39–'45 war*, but write instead *the 1939–45 war*.

5.2 Unusual Plurals

As a general rule, we **never** use an apostrophe in writing plural forms. (A plural form is one that denotes more than one of something.) Hence the things that those shops are selling are *pizzas*, *videos*, *fine wines*, *cream teas* and *mountain bikes*. It is absolutely **wrong** to write ★ *pizza's*, ★ *video's*,★ *fine wine's*, ★ *cream tea's* and ★ *mountain bike's* if you merely want to talk about more than one pizza or video or whatever. The same goes even when you want to pluralize a proper name:

She's trying to keep up with the Joneses.
There are four Steves and three Julies in my class.
Several of the Eleanor Crosses are still standing today.

Do **not** write things like ★*Jones's*, ★ *Steve's*, ★*Julie's* or ★ *Eleanor Cross's* if you are merely talking about more than one person or thing with that name.

In British usage, we do not use an apostrophe in pluralizing dates:

This research was carried out in the 1970s.

American usage, however, does put an apostrophe here:

(A) This research was carried out in the 1970's.

You should **not** adopt this practice unless you are specifically writing for an American audience.

In writing the plurals of numbers, usage varies. Both of the following may be encountered:

If you're sending mail to the Continent, it's advisable to use continental *1*s and *7*s in the address.
If you're sending mail to the Continent, it's advisable to use continental *1*'s and *7*'s in the address.

Here, the first form is admittedly a little hard on the eye, and the apostrophes may make your sentence clearer. In most cases, though, you can avoid the problem entirely simply by writing out the numerals:

If you're sending mail to the Continent, it's advisable to use continental ones and sevens in the address.

An apostrophe is indispensable, however, in the rare case in which you need to pluralize a letter of the alphabet or some other unusual form which would become unrecognizable with a plural ending stuck on it:

Mind your *p*'s and *q*'s.
How many *s*'s are there in *Mississippi*?
It is very bad style to spatter *e.g.*'s and *i.e.*'s through your writing.

Without the apostrophes, these would be unreadable. So, when you have to pluralize an orthographically unusual form, use an apostrophe if it seems to be essential for clarity, but **don't** use one if the written form is perfectly clear without it. (Note that I have italicized these odd forms; this is a very good practice if you can produce italics. See Chapter 9.)

5.3 Possessives

An apostrophe is used in a possessive form, like *Esther's family* or *Janet's cigarettes*, and this is the use of the apostrophe which causes most of the trouble. The basic rule is simple enough: a possessive form is spelled with *'s* at the end. Hence:

Lisa's essay	England's navy
my brother's girlfriend	Wittgenstein's last book
children's shoes	women's clothing
the aircraft's black box	somebody's umbrella
a week's work	my money's worth

This rule applies in most cases even with a name ending in *s*:

Thomas's job	the bus's arrival
James's fiancée	Steve Davis's victory

There are three types of exception. First, a plural noun which already ends in *s* takes only a following apostrophe:

the girls' excitement	my parents' wedding
both players' injuries	the Klingons' attack
the ladies' room	two weeks' work

This is reasonable. We don't pronounce these words with two esses, and so we don't write two esses: nobody says ★ *the girls's excitement*. But note that plurals that don't end in *s* take the ordinary form: see the cases of *children* and *women* above.

Second, a name ending in *s* takes only an apostrophe if the possessive form is not pronounced with an extra *s*. Hence:

Socrates' philosophy	Saint Saens' music
Ulysses' companions	Aristophanes' plays

Same reason: we don't say ★ *Ulysses's companions*, and so we don't write the extra *s*.

The final class of exceptions is pronouns. Note the following:

He lost his book	Which seats are ours?
The bull lowered its head.	Whose are these spectacles?

Note in particular the spelling of possessive *its*. This word never takes an apostrophe:

★ The bull lowered it's head

This is **wrong, wrong, wrong** – but it is one of the commonest of all punctuation errors. I have even met teachers of English who get this wrong. The conventional spelling *its* is no doubt totally illogical, but it's none the less conventional, and spelling the possessive as *it's* will cause many readers to turn up their noses at you. The mistake is very conspicuous, but fortunately it's also easy to fix – there's only one word – so learn the standard spelling. (There is an English word spelled *it's*, of course, and indeed I've just used it in the preceding sentence, but this is not a possessive: it's the contracted form of *it is* or of *it has*. And there is **no** English word spelled ★ *its'* – this is another common error for *its*.)

The same goes for possessive *whose*: this cannot be spelled as ★ *who's*, though again there is a word *who's*, a contraction of *who is* or of *who has*, as in *Who's your friend?* or *Who's got a corkscrew?*

Note, however, that the indefinite pronoun *one* forms an ordinary possessive *one's*, as in *One must choose one's words carefully*.

There is a further point about writing possessives: when you add an apostrophe-*s* or an apostrophe alone to form a possessive, the thing that comes before the apostrophe *must* be a real English word, and it must also be the *right* English word. Thus, for example, something like ★ *ladie's shoes* is impossible, because there is no such word as ★ *ladie*. Moreover, a department in a shoeshop could not be called ★ *lady's shoes*, because what the shop is selling is *shoes for ladies*, and not ★ *shoes for lady*, which is meaningless. The correct form is *ladies' shoes*. (Compare *that lady's shoes*, which is fine.)

Finally, while we're discussing clothing departments, observe that there is at least one irritating exception: though we write *men's clothing*, as usual, we write *menswear* as a single word, with no apostrophe. By historical accident, this has come to be regarded as a single word in English. But just this one: we do **not** write ★ *womenswear* or ★ *childrenswear*. Sorry.

Chapter 6
The Hyphen and the Dash

6.1 The Hyphen

The **hyphen** (-) is the small bar found on every keyboard. It has several related uses; in every case, it is used to show that what it is attached to does not make up a complete word by itself. The hyphen must **never** be used with white spaces at both ends, though in some uses it may have a white space at one end.

Most obviously, a hyphen is used to indicate that a long word has been broken off at the end of a line:

> We were dismayed at having to listen to such inconse-
> quential remarks.

You should avoid such word splitting whenever possible. If it is unavoidable, try to split the word into two roughly equal parts, and make sure you split it at an obvious boundary. Do not write things like:

★ incons- equential	★ inconseque- ntial	★ inconsequent- ial

The first two of these are not broken at syllable boundaries, while the third is broken into two very unequal pieces. If you are in doubt as to where a word can be split, consult a dictionary. Many good dictionaries mark syllable boundaries to show you where words can be hyphenated. Some publishers even bring out hyphenation dictionaries containing no other information. Best of all, many word processors will perform hyphenation automatically, and you won't have to worry about it. In any case, note that a hyphen in such a case must be written at the end of its line, and not at the beginning of the following line.

The hyphen is also used in writing compound words which, without the hyphen, would be ambiguous, hard to read or overly long. Here, more than anywhere else in the whole field of punctuation, there is room for individual taste and judgement; nevertheless, certain principles may be identified. These are:

1. Above all, strive for clarity;
2. Don't use a hyphen unless it's necessary;
3. Where possible, follow established usage.

On this last point, consult a good dictionary; Collins or Longman is recommended, since the conservative Chambers and Oxford dictionaries frequently show hyphens which are no longer in normal use.

Should you write *land owners*, *land-owners* or *landowners*? All are possible, and you should follow your judgement, and

British usage generally favours rather more hyphens here than does American usage; nevertheless, I prefer the third, since it seems unambiguous and easy to read, since it avoids the use of a hyphen and since this form is confirmed by Longman and Collins as the usual one (while Chambers, predictably, insists on the hyphenated form).

What about *electro-magnetic* versus *electromagnetic*? Collins and Longman confirm that only the second is in use among those who use the term regularly, but Oxford clings stubbornly to the antiquated and pointless hyphen.

On the other hand, things like ★ *pressurecooker*, ★ *wordprocessor* and ★ *emeraldgreen* are impossibly hard on the eye; reference to a good dictionary will confirm that the established forms of the first two are *pressure cooker* and *word processor*, while the last is *emerald green* or *emerald-green*, depending on how it is used (see below).

The hyphen is regularly used in writing so-called 'double-barrelled' names: *José-María Olazábal*, *Jean-Paul Gaultier*, *Claude Lévi-Strauss*, *Philip Johnson-Laird*. However, some individuals with such names prefer to omit the hyphen: *Jean Paul Sartre*, *Hillary Rodham Clinton*. You should always respect the usage of the owner of the name.

Now here is something important: it is usually essential to hyphenate compound modifiers. Compare the following:

She kissed him good night.
She gave him a good-night kiss.

The hyphen in the second example is necessary to show

that *good-night* is a single compound modifier. Without the hyphen, the reader might easily be misled:

★ She gave him a good night kiss.

Here the reader might be momentarily flummoxed into thinking that she had given him some kind of *'night kiss'*, whatever that means. Here are some further examples:

Her dress is light green.
She's wearing a light-green dress.

This book token is worth ten pounds.
This is a ten-pound book token.

She always turned up for the parties at the end of term.
She always turned up for the end-of-term parties.

This essay is well thought out.
This is a well-thought-out essay.

Her son is ten years old.
She has a ten-year-old son.

Use hyphens liberally in such compound modifiers; they are often vital to comprehension: *a light-green dress* is not necessarily *a light green dress*; *our first-class discussion* is quite different from *our first class discussion*; *a rusty-nail cutter* is hardly the same as *a rusty nail-cutter; a woman-hating religion* is utterly different from *a woman hating religion*; and *a nude-review producer* is most unlikely to be *a nude review producer*! You can mislead your reader disastrously by omitting these crucial hyphens: *She always turned up for the end of term parties* does not appear to mean the same as the hyphenated example above (example adapted from Carey 1958: 82). So make a habit of hyphenating your compound modifiers:

a long-standing friend	*not*	* a long standing friend
well-defined rules	*not*	* well defined rules
a copper-producing region	*not*	* a copper producing region
a low-scoring match	*not*	* a low scoring match
little-expected news	*not*	* little expected news
a green-eyed beauty	*not*	* a green eyed beauty
a rough-and-ready approach	*not*	* a rough and ready approach
a salt-and-pepper moustache	*not*	* a salt and pepper moustache
a far-ranging investigation	*not*	* a far ranging investigation
her Swiss-German ancestry	*not*	* her Swiss German ancestry
her new-found freedom	*not*	* her new found freedom
the hang-'em-and-flog-'em brigade	*not*	* the hang 'em and flog 'em brigade

The correct use or non-use of a hyphen in a modifier can be of vital importance in making your meaning clear. Consider the next two examples:

The earliest known hominid was *Homo habilis*.

The earliest-known hominid was *Homo habilis*.

These do not mean the same thing at all. The first means that, of all the hominids we know about, *H. habilis* was the earliest one to exist (but not necessarily the first one we knew about). The second means that, of all the hominids, *H. Habilis* was the first one we knew about (but not necessarily the first one to exist). Effectively, the first sentence includes the structure [*earliest*] [*known hominid*], while the second includes the structure [*earliest-known*] [*hominid*]. Again, these two sentences would be pronounced differently, but the pronunciation difference is lost in writing; hence accurate punctuation is essential if you are not going to mislead your reader utterly. Punctuation is not a matter for personal taste and caprice, not if you want your readers to understand what you've written. (As it happens, the first statement is true, but the second one is false.)

A compound modifier may also require a hyphen when it appears after the verb. Here is a splendid example from Carey (1958): *Her face turned an ugly brick-red* appears to mean something very different from *Her face turned an ugly brick red*.

Old-fashioned usage, especially in Britain, favours excessive hyphenation, producing such forms as *to-day*, *co-operate*, *ski-ing*, *semi-colon* and even *full-stop*; such hyphens are pointless and ugly and should be avoided. Much better are *today*, *cooperate*, *skiing*, *semicolon* and *full stop*: don't use a hyphen unless it's doing some real work.

Prefixes present special problems. *She's repainting the lounge* seems unobjectionable, but *She's reliving her childhood* is possibly hard to read and should perhaps be rewritten as *She's re-living her childhood.* And *She re-covered the sofa* [= 'She put a new cover on the sofa'] is absolutely essential to avoid confusion with the entirely different *She recovered the sofa* [= 'She got the sofa back']. The chemical term meaning 'not ionized' is routinely written by chemists as *unionized*, but, in some contexts, you might prefer to write *un-ionized* to avoid possible confusion with the unrelated word *unionized* 'organized into unions'. Use your judgement: put a hyphen in if you can see a problem without it, but otherwise leave it out. Here are a few examples of good usage:

miniskirt	*but*	mini-aircraft
nonviolent	*but*	non-negotiable
prejudge	*but*	pre-empt
antisocial	*but*	anti-aircraft

The hyphen is written only when the word would be hard to read without it: ★ *nonnegotiable*, ★ *preempt*. As always, consult a good dictionary if you're not sure.

Observe, by the way, that a prefix must **not** be written as though it were a separate word. Thus all the following are **wrong**:

★ post war period
★ mini computer
★ non communist countries
★ anti vivisectionists

There are three cases in which a hyphen is absolutely required after a prefix. First, if a capital letter or a numeral follows:

non-EC countries	un-American activities
pre-Newtonian physics	anti-French feeling
post-Napoleonic Europe	pre-1500 English literature

Second, if the prefix is added to a word which already contains a hyphen:

non-bribe-taking politicians	his pre-globe-trotting days
non-stress-timed languages	an un-re-elected politician

Your reader cannot be expected to take in at a glance some indigestible glob like ★ *his preglobe-trotting days* or ★ *an unre-elected politician.*

Third, if the prefix is added to a compound word containing a white space. In this case, the white space itself must be replaced by a hyphen to prevent the prefixed word from becoming unreadable:

seal killing	*but*	anti-seal-killing campaigners
twentieth century	*but*	pre-twentieth-century music
cold war	*but*	our post-cold-war world

Again, your readers will not thank you for writing something like ★ *antiseal-killing campaigners* or ★ *our postcold-war world* (or, still worse, ★ *our postcold war world*, a piece of gibberish I recently encountered in a major newspaper). Who are these campaigners who kill *antiseals*, whatever those might be, and what is a *war world* and what is special about a *postcold* one?

In any case, do not go overboard with large and complex modifiers. The cumbersome *anti-seal-killing campaigners* can easily be replaced by *campaigners against seal killing*, which is much easier to read.

Finally, the hyphen has one rather special use: it is used in writing pieces of words. Here are some examples:

The prefix *re*– sometimes requires a hyphen.

The suffix -*wise*, as in 'moneywise' and 'healthwise', has become enormously popular in recent years.

The Latin word *rex* 'king' has a stem *reg*-.

Only when you are writing about language are you likely to need this use of the hyphen. If you do use it, make sure you put the hyphen at the correct end of the piece-of-a-word you are citing – that is, the end at which the piece has to be connected to something else to make a word. And note that, when you're writing a suffix, the hyphen must go on the same line as the suffix itself: you should not allow the hyphen to stand at the end of its line, with the suffix on the next line. Word processors won't do this automatically, and you will need to consult your manual to find out how to type a *hard hyphen*, which will always stay where it belongs.

There is, however, one very special case in which you might want to write a piece of a word in any kind of text. Consider the following example:

Pre-war and post-war Berlin could hardly be more different.

There is another way of writing this:

Pre- and post-war Berlin could hardly be more different.

This style is permissible, but observe that the now isolated prefix *pre-* requires a hyphen, since it is only a piece of a word.

The same thing happens when you want to write a piece of a word which is not normally hyphenated, in order to avoid repetition:

Natalie is studying sociolinguistics and psycholinguistics.

This can also be written as follows:

Natalie is studying socio- and psycholinguistics.

The use of the hyphen in writing numerals and fractions is covered in Chapter 9.

6.2 The Dash

The **dash** (–) is the long horizontal bar, noticeably longer than a hyphen. Few keyboards have a dash, but a word processor can usually produce one in one way or another. If your keyboard can't produce a dash, you will have to resort to a hyphen as a stand-in. In British usage, we use only a single hyphen to represent a dash - like this. American usage, in contrast, uses two consecutive hyphens -- like this (A). Here I must confess that I strongly prefer the American style, since the double hyphen is far more prominent than a single one and avoids any possibility of ambiguity. If you are writing for publication, you will probably have to use the single hyphen; in other contexts, you should consider using the more vivid double hyphen. In any case, you will be very unlucky if your word processor can't produce a proper dash and save you from worrying about this.

The dash has only one major use: a **pair** of dashes separates a strong interruption from the rest of the sentence. (A strong interruption is one which violently disrupts the flow of the sentence.) Again, note that word 'pair': in principle, at least, dashes come in pairs, though sometimes one of them is not written. (Remember that the same thing is true of bracketing commas, which set off weak interruptions.) Here are some examples:

An honest politician – if such a creature exists – would never agree to such a plan.

The destruction of Guernica – and there is no doubt that the destruction was deliberate – horrified the world.

When the Europeans settled in Tasmania, they inflicted genocide – there is no other word for it – upon the indigenous population, who were wiped out in thirty years.

If the strong interruption comes at the end of the sentence, then of course only one dash is used:

The Serbs want peace – or so they say.

In 1453 Sultan Mehmed finally took Constantinople –

and the Byzantine Empire disappeared from the map for ever.

There was no other way – or was there?

In the case in which the original sentence is never resumed after the interruption, only one dash is used:

John, do you suppose you could – oh, never mind; I'll do it.

This sort of broken sentence is only found in representations of conversation, such as you might find in a novel; it is never appropriate in formal writing.

Finally, in the rare case in which a sentence is broken off abruptly without being completed, a single dash is also used:

General Sedgwick's last words to his worried staff were 'Don't worry, boys; they couldn't hit an elephant at this dist–'.

Note that, in this case, the dash is written solid next to the unfinished piece-of-a-word which precedes it. (If the sentence merely tails off into silence, we use, not a dash, but an ellipsis; see section 9.6.)

When a dash falls between the end of one line and the beginning of the next, you should try to ensure that the dash is placed at the end of the first line and not at the beginning of the second, if you can. Most words processors will not do this automatically, however, and it will require some fiddling.

The dash is also used in representing ranges of numbers, and occasionally also other ranges. A representation of the form *X–Y* means 'from *X* to *Y*' or 'between *X* and *Y*'. Here are some examples:

Steel contains 0.1–1.7% carbon.
These fossils are 30–35 million years old.
The London–Brighton vintage car rally takes place on Sunday.
The declaration of the Rome–Berlin axis led to the use of the label 'Axis powers' for Germany and Italy.

Do **not** write things like this:

★ Steel contains from 0.1–1.7% carbon.
★ Steel contains between 0.1–1.7% carbon.

These are terrible, since the sense of 'from' or 'between' is already included in the punctuation. If you prefer to use words, then write the words out in full, with no dashes:

Steel contains from 0.1 to 1.7% carbon.
Steel contains between 0.1 and 1.7% carbon.

And, of course, do not tangle up these two constructions:

★ Steel contains between 0.1 to 1.7% carbon.

A construction of the form ★ *between X to Y* is always wrong. Similarly, do **not** write things like this:

★ She was living in Rome from 1977–83.

Instead, write the dates out in full:

She was living in Rome from 1977 to 1983.

That's all there is to know about the dash. Use the dash carefully: overuse of dashes will give your writing a breathless and disjointed appearance. And don't use a dash for any purpose other than setting off a strong interruption or marking a range: the dash is **never** used in place of a hyphen, after a colon or after a heading. It is not used to introduce a direct quotation, except sometimes in novels, but this is not a usage you should imitate.

There is one last point, very trivial. In a certain style of writing which is now felt to be antique and genteel, an extra-long dash is occasionally used to represent the omission of several letters from a word or a name. The exceedingly genteel Victorian novelists often wrote *d—n* in place of *damn*, and even *Go to the d—l!* instead of *Go to the devil!* Such usages strike us as comical now, and few writers today would hesitate to write out such mild oaths in full (but compare the related use of asterisks in section 9.10 for the coarser words). Some Victorians, not wanting to set their fictional narratives in any identifiable location, also wrote things like *At the time, I was living at B— in the county of S—*. This quaint affectation is now dead.

Chapter 7

Capital Letters and Abbreviations

7.1 Capital Letters

Capital letters are not really an aspect of punctuation, but it is convenient to deal with them here. The rules for using them are mostly very simple.

(**a**) The first word of a sentence, or of a fragment, begins with a capital letter:

> The bumbling wizard Rincewind is Pratchett's most popular character.
> Will anyone now alive live to see a colony on the moon? Probably not.
> Distressingly few pupils can locate Iraq or Japan on a map of the world.

(**b**) The names of the days of the week, and of the months of the year, are written with a capital letter:

> Next Sunday France will hold a general election.
> Mozart was born on 27 January 1756.
> Football practice takes place on Wednesdays and Fridays.

However, the names of seasons are **not** written with a capital:

Like cricket, baseball is played in the summer.

Do not write ★ . . . *in the Summer.*

(**c**) The names of languages are always written with a capital letter. Be careful about this; it's a very common mistake.

Juliet speaks English, French, Italian and Portuguese.
I need to work on my Spanish irregular verbs.
Among the major languages of India are Hindi, Gujarati and Tamil.
These days, few students study Latin and Greek.

Note, however, that names of disciplines and school subjects are **not** capitalized unless they happen to be the names of languages:

I'm doing A levels in history, geography and English.
Newton made important contributions to physics and mathematics.
She is studying French literature.

(**d**) Words that express a connection with a particular place must be capitalized when they have their literal meanings. So, for example, *French* must be capitalized when it means 'having to do with France':

The result of the French election is still in doubt.
The American and Russian negotiators are close to agreement.

There are no mountains in the Dutch landscape.

She has a dry Mancunian sense of humour.

(The word *Mancunian* means 'from Manchester'.)

However, it is not necessary to capitalize these words when they occur as parts of fixed phrases and don't express any direct connection with the relevant places:

Please buy some danish pastries.

In warm weather, we keep our french windows open.

I prefer russian dressing on my salad.

Why the difference? Well, a danish pastry is merely a particular sort of pastry; it doesn't have to come from Denmark. Likewise, french windows are merely a particular kind of window, and russian dressing is just a particular varietyof salad dressing. Even in these cases, you can capitalize these words if you want to, as long as you are consistent about it. But notice how convenient it can be to make the difference:

In warm weather, we keep our french windows open.

After nightfall, French windows are always shuttered.

In the first example, *french windows* just refers to a kind of window; in the second, *French windows* refers specifically to windows in France.

(e) In the same vein, words that identify nationalities or ethnic groups must be capitalized:

The Basques and the Catalans spent decades struggling for autonomy.

The Serbs and the Croats have become bitter enemies.
Norway's most popular singer is a Sami from Lapland.

(An aside: some ethnic labels which were formerly widely used are now regarded by many people as offensive and have been replaced by other labels. Thus, careful writers use *Black*, or *Afro-Caribbean*, not *Negro*, in Britain (but *African-American*, not *Black*, in the USA); *native American*, not *Indian* or *red Indian*; *native Australian*, not *Aborigine* (though *Aboriginal* is still just about acceptable, but probably not for long). You are advised to follow suit.)

(**f**) Formerly, the words *black* and *white*, when applied to human beings, were never capitalized. Nowadays, however, many people prefer to capitalize them because they regard these words as ethnic labels comparable to *Chinese* or *Indian*:

The Rodney King case infuriated many Black Americans.

You may capitalize these words or not, as you prefer, but be consistent.

(**g**) Proper names are always capitalized. A proper name is a name or a title that refers to an individual person, an individual place, an individual institution or an individual event. Here are some examples:

The study of language was revolutionized by Noam Chomsky.
The Golden Gate Bridge towers above San Francisco Bay.

There will be a debate between Professor Lacey and Doctor Davis.
The Queen will address the House of Commons today.
Many people mistakenly believe that Mexico is in South America.
My friend Julie is training for the Winter Olympics.
Next week President Clinton will be meeting Chancellor Kohl.

Observe the difference between the next two examples:

We have asked for a meeting with the President.
I would like to be the president of a big company.

In the first, the title *the President* is capitalized because it is a title referring to a specific person; in the second, there is no capital, because the word *president* does not refer to anyone in particular. (Compare *We have asked for a meeting with President Wilson* and ★ *I would like to be President Wilson of a big company.*) The same difference is made with some other words: we write *the Government* and *Parliament* when we are referring to a particular government or a particular parliament, but we write *government* and *parliament* when we are using the words generically. And note also the following example:

The patron saint of carpenters is Saint Joseph.

Here *Saint Joseph* is a name, but *patron saint* is not and gets no capital.

There is a slight problem with the names of hazily defined geographical regions. We usually write *the Middle East* and

Southeast Asia, because these regions are now regarded as having a distinctive identity, but we write *central Europe* and *southeast London*, because these regions are not thought of as having the same kind of identity. Note, too, the difference between *South Africa* (the name of a particular country) and *southern Africa* (a vaguely defined region). All I can suggest here is that you read a good newspaper and keep your eyes open.

Observe that certain surnames of foreign origin contain little words that are often not capitalized, such as *de*, *du*, *da*, *von* and *van*. Thus we write *Leonardo da Vinci*, *Ludwig van Beethoven*, *General von Moltke* and *Simone de Beauvoir*. On the other hand, we write *Daphne Du Maurier* and *Dick Van Dyke*, because those are the forms preferred by the owners of the names. When in doubt, check the spelling in a good reference book.

A few people eccentrically prefer to write their names with no capital letters at all, such as the poet *e. e. cummings* and the singer *k. d. lang*. These strange usages should be respected.

(**h**) The names of distinctive historical periods are capitalized:

London was a prosperous city during the Middle Ages.
Britain was the first country to profit from the Industrial Revolution.
The Greeks were already in Greece during the Bronze Age.

(**i**) The names of festivals and holy days are capitalized:

We have long breaks at Christmas and Easter.

During Ramadan, one may not eat before sundown.
The feast of Purim is an occasion for merrymaking.
Our church observes the Sabbath very strictly.
The children greatly enjoy Hallowe'en.

(**j**) Many religious terms are capitalized, including the names of religions and of their followers, the names or titles of divine beings, the titles of certain important figures, the names of important events and the names of sacred books:

An atheist is a person who does not believe in God.
The principal religions of Japan are Shinto and Buddhism.
The Indian cricket team includes Hindus, Muslims, Sikhs and Parsees.
The Lord is my shepherd.
The Prophet was born in Mecca.
The Last Supper took place on the night before the Crucifixion.
The Old Testament begins with Genesis.

Note, however, that the word *god* is **not** capitalized when it refers to a pagan deity:

Poseidon was the Greek god of the sea.

(**k**) In the title or name of a book, a play, a poem, a film, a magazine, a newspaper or a piece of music, a capital letter is used for the first word and for every significant word (that is, a little word like *the*, *of*, *and* or *in* is not capitalized unless it is the first word):

I was terrified by *The Silence of the Lambs.*

The Round Tower was written by Catherine Cookson.

Bach's most famous organ piece is the *Toccata and Fugue in D Minor.*

I don't usually like Cher, but I do enjoy 'The Shoop Shoop Song'.

Important note: The policy just described is the one most widely used in the English-speaking world. There is, however, a second policy, preferred by many people. In this second policy, we capitalize only the first word of a title and any words which intrinsically require capitals for independent reasons. Using the second policy, my examples would look lke this:

I was terrified by *The silence of the lambs.*

The round tower was written by Catherine Cookson.

Bach's most famous organ piece is the *Toccata and fugue in D minor.*

I don't usually like Cher, but I do enjoy 'The shoop shoop song'.

You may use whichever policy you prefer, so long as you are consistent about it. You may find, however, that your tutor or your editor insists upon one or the other. The second policy is particularly common (though not universal) in academic circles, and is usual among librarians; elsewhere, the first policy is almost always preferred.

(**l**) The first word of a direct quotation, repeating someone else's exact words, is always capitalized if the quotation is a complete sentence:

> Thomas Edison famously observed, 'Genius is one per cent inspiration and ninety-nine per cent perspiration.'

But there is no capital letter if the quotation is not a complete sentence:

> The Minister described the latest unemployment figures as 'disappointing'.

(m) The brand names of manufacturers and their products are capitalized:

> Maxine has bought a second-hand Ford Escort.
> Almost everybody owns a Sony Walkman.

Note: There is a problem with brand names which have become so successful that they are used in ordinary speech as generic labels for classes of products. The manufacturers of *Kleenex* and *Sellotape* are exasperated to find people using *kleenex* and *sellotape* as ordinary words for facial tissues or sticky tape of any kind, and some such manufacturers may actually take legal action against this practice. If you are writing for publication, you need to be careful about this, and it is best to capitalize such words if you use them. However, when brand names are converted into verbs, no capital letter is used: we write *She was hoovering the carpet* and *I need to xerox this report*, even though the manufacturers of *Hoover* vacuum cleaners and *Xerox* photocopiers don't much like this practice, either.

(**n**) Roman numerals are usually capitalized:

> It is no easy task to multiply LIX by XXIV using roman numerals.
> King Alfonso XIII handed over power to General Primo de Rivera.

The only common exception is that small roman numerals are used to number the pages of the front matter in books; look at almost any book.

(**o**) The pronoun *I* is always capitalized:

> She thought I'd borrowed her keys, but I hadn't.

It is possible to write an entire word or phrase in capital letters in order to emphasize it:

> There is ABSOLUTELY NO EVIDENCE to support this conjecture.

On the whole, though, it is preferable to express emphasis, not with capital letters, but with italics, as explained in Chapter 9.

It is not necessary to capitalize a word merely because there is only one thing it can possibly refer to:

> The equator runs through the middle of Brazil.
> Admiral Peary was the first person to fly over the north pole.
> The universe is thought to be about 15 billion years old.

Here the words *equator, north pole* and *universe* need no capitals, because they aren't strictly proper names. Some people choose to capitalize them anyway; this is not wrong, but it's not recommended.

The use of capital letters in writing certain abbreviations and related types of words, including the abbreviated names of organizations and companies, is explained in the next section; the use of capital letters in letter-writing and in the headings of essays is explained in Chapter 10.

There is one other rather rare use of capital letters which is worth explaining if only to prevent you from doing it by mistake when you don't mean to. This is to poke fun at something. Here is an example:

> The French Revolution was a Good Thing at first, but Napoleon's rise to power was a Bad Thing.

Here the writer is making fun of the common tendency to see historical events in simple-minded terms as either good or bad. Another example:

> Many people claim that rock music is Serious Art, deserving of Serious Critical Attention.

The writer is clearly being sarcastic: all those unusual capital letters demonstrate that he considers rock music to be worthless trash.

This stylistic device is only appropriate in writing which is intended to be humorous, or at least light-hearted; it is quite out of place in formal writing.

The use of unnecessary capital letters when you're trying to be serious can quickly make your prose look idiotic, rather like those content-free books that fill the shelves of the New Age section in bookshops:

> Your Eidetic Soul is linked by its Crystal Cord to the Seventh Circle of the Astral Plane, from where the Immanent Essence is transmitted to your Eidetic Aura . . .

You get the idea. **Don't** use a capital letter unless you're sure you know why it's there.

Summary of capital letters

Capitalize

- **the first word of a sentence or fragment**
- **the name of a day or a month**
- **the name of a language**
- **a word expressing a connection with a place**
- **the name of a nationality or an ethnic group**
- **a proper name**
- **the name of a historical period**
- **the name of a holiday**
- **a significant religious term**
- **the first word, and each significant word, of a title**
- **the first word of a direct quotation which is a sentence**
- **a brand name**
- **a roman numeral**
- **the pronoun *I***

7.2 Abbreviations

An **abbreviation** is a short way of writing a word or a phrase that could also be written out in full. So, for example, you might write *Dr Kinsey* instead of *Doctor Kinsey*. Here *Dr* is an abbreviation for the word *Doctor*. Likewise, the phrase *for example* can sometimes be abbreviated to *e.g.*

Abbreviations must be clearly distinguished from *contractions*, which were discussed in section 5.1. The key difference is that an abbreviation does not *normally* have a distinctive pronunciation of its own. So, for example, the abbreviation *Dr* is pronounced just like *Doctor*, the abbreviation *oz.* is pronounced just like *ounce(s)* and the abbreviation *e.g.* is pronounced just like *for example.* (True, there are a few people who actually say 'ee-jee' for the last one, but this practice is decidedly unusual.) A contraction, in contrast, *does* have its own distinctive pronunciation: for example, the contraction *can't* is pronounced differently from *cannot*, and the contraction *she's* is pronounced differently from *she is* or *she has*.

Abbreviations are very rarely used in formal writing. Almost the only ones which are frequently used are the abbreviations for certain common titles, when these are used with someone's name: *Mr Willis, Dr Livingstone, Mrs Thatcher, Ms Harmon, St Joan.* (Note that the two items *Mrs* and *Ms* are conventionally treated as abbreviations, even though they can be written in no other way.) When writing about a French or Spanish person, you may use the abbreviations for the

French and Spanish equivalents of the English titles: *M. Mitterrand*, *Sr. González*. (These are the usual French and Spanish abbreviations for *Monsieur* and *Señor*, equivalent to English *Mister*.) Observe that each of these abbreviations begins with a capital letter.

Other titles are sometimes abbreviated in the same way: *Prof. Chomsky*, *Sgt. Yorke*, *Mgr. Lindemann*. However, it is usually much better to write these titles out in full when you are using them in a sentence: *Professor Chomsky*, *Sergeant Yorke*, *Monsignor Lindemann*. The abbreviated forms are best confined to places like footnotes and captions of pictures.

Note carefully the use of full stops in these abbreviations. British usage favours omitting the full stop in abbreviations which include the first and last letters of a single word, such as *Mr*, *Mrs*, *Ms*, *Dr* and *St*; American usage prefers (A) *Mr.*, *Mrs.*, *Ms.*, *Dr.* and *St.*, with full stops. Most other abbreviated titles, however, require a full stop, as shown above.

A person's initials are a kind of abbreviation, and these are usually followed by full stops: *John D. Rockefeller*, *C. Aubrey Smith*, *O. J. Simpson*. Increasingly, however, there is a tendency to write such initials without full stops: *John D Rockefeller*, *C Aubrey Smith*, *O J Simpson*. And note the rare special case illustrated by *Harry S Truman*: the *S* in this name never takes a full stop, because it's not an abbreviation for anything; President Truman's parents actually gave him the middle name *S*.

Two other common abbreviations are *a.m.* ('before noon') and *p.m.* ('after noon'): *10.00 a.m.*, *six p.m.* These are always acceptable. Note that these are not capitalized in British usage (though American usage prefers (A) *10:00 AM* and *six PM*, with small capitals and no full stops).

Also usual are the abbreviations *BC* and *AD*, usually written in small capitals, for marking dates as before or after the birth of Christ:

According to tradition, Rome was founded in 753 BC.
The emperor Vespasian died in AD 79. **or**
The emperor Vespasian died in 79 AD.

It is traditional, and recommended, to write *AD* before the date, but nowadays it is often written after.

Non-Christians who do not use the Christian calendar may prefer to use *BCE* ('before the common era') and *CE* ('of the common era') instead. This is always acceptable:

According to tradition, Rome was founded in 753 BCE.
The emperor Vespasian died in 79 CE.

All four of these abbreviations are commonly written in small capitals, and you should follow this practice if you can; if you can't produce small capitals, use full-sized capitals instead.

Note also that, when an abbreviation comes at the end of a sentence, only one full stop is written. You should **never** write two full stops in a row.

Many large and well-known organizations and companies have very long names which are commonly abbreviated to a set of initials written in capital letters, usually with no full stops. Here are a few familiar examples:

BBC	British Broadcasting Corporation
ICI	Imperial Chemical Industries
FBI	Federal Bureau of Investigation
RSPCA	Royal Society for the Prevention of Cruelty to Animals
NATO	North Atlantic Treaty Organization
MIT	Massachusetts Institute of Technology
TUC	Trades Union Congress

These and some others are so famous that you can safely use the abbreviated forms without explanation. But don't overdo it – not every reader will recognize *IRO* as the International Refugee Organization, or *IOOF* as the Independent Order of Odd Fellows (an American social and charitable organization). And, if you're writing for a non-British readership, you'd better not use the abbreviated forms of specifically British institutions, such as the *TUC*, without explaining them. If you are in doubt, explain the abbreviation the first time you use it. (Note that a few of these were formerly written with full stops, such as *R.S.P.C.A.*, but this tiresome and unnecessary practice is now obsolete.)

A few other abbreviations are so well known that you can use them safely in your writing. Every reader will understand what you mean by *GCSE examinations* (*GCSE* = *General Certificate of Secondary Education*), or by *DDT* (*dichlorodiphenyltrichloroethane*), or by *IQ* (*intelligence quotient*), or by *FM radio* (*FM* = *frequency modulation*). Indeed, in some of these cases, the abbreviated form of the name is far more familiar than the full name.

Otherwise, however, you should try to avoid the use of abbreviations in your formal writing. The frequent use of unnecessary abbreviations will make your text irritating and hard to read. So, you should write *four ounces* (**not** *4 oz.*), *80 miles per hour* (**not** *80 mph*), *the Church of England* (**not** *the C of E*), *the seventeenth century* (**not** *C17* or *the 17th cent.*) and *the second volume* (**not** *the 2nd vol.*). It is far more important to make your writing easy to read than to save a few seconds in writing it.

There is one exception to this policy. In scientific writing, the names of units are always abbreviated and always written without full stops or a plural *s*. If you are doing scientific writing, then, you should conform by writing *5 kg* (**not** *5 kilogrammes*, and certainly not * *5 kg.* or * *5 kgs.*), *800 Hz* (**not** *800 Hertz*) and *17.3 cm*^{3} (**not** *17.3 cubic centimetres*).

There are a number of Latin abbreviations which are sometimes used in English texts. Here are the commonest ones with their English equivalents:

e.g.	for example
i.e.	in other words
viz.	namely
sc.	which means
c.	approximately
cf.	compare
v.	consult
etc.	and so forth
et al.	and other people

The rule about using these Latin abbreviations is very simple: **don't use them**. Their use is only appropriate in special circumstances in which brevity is at a premium, such as in footnotes. It is very poor style to spatter your page with these things, and it could be disastrous to use them without being quite sure what they mean. If you do use one, make sure you punctuate it correctly. Here is an example. The recommended form is this:

> Several British universities were founded in the Victorian era; for example, the University of Manchester was established in 1851.

The following version is not wrong, but it is poor style:

> Several British universities were founded in the Victorian era; e.g., the University of Manchester was established in 1851.

But this next version is disastrously wrong, because the punctuation has been omitted:

> * Several British universities were founded in the Victorian era e.g. the University of Manchester was established in 1851.

Using a Latin abbreviation does not relieve you of the obligation of punctuating your sentence. Again, if you avoid Latin abbreviations, you won't get into this sort of trouble.

The abbreviation *c.* 'approximately' is properly used only in citing a date which is not known exactly, and then usually only if the date is given in parentheses:

The famous Basque cemetery of Argiñeta in Elorrio (*c.* AD 883) shows tombs with sun-discs but no crosses.
Roger Bacon (*c.* 1214–94) was known as 'the Admirable Doctor'.

Here the use of *c.* shows that the date of the cemetery and the date of Bacon's birth are not known exactly. If neither birth date nor death date is known for sure, then each is preceded by *c.*

Outside of parentheses, you should usually avoid the use of *c.* and prefer an English word like *about* or *approximately*:

The city of Bilbao was founded in about 1210.

Do not write '*. . . in* c. *1210*'.

The abbreviation *etc.* calls for special comment. It should **never** be used in careful writing: it is vague and sloppy and, when applied to people, rather offensive. **Do not** write something like this:

* Central Africa was explored by Livingstone, Stanley, Brazza, etc.

Instead, rewrite the sentence in a more explicit way:

Central Africa was explored by Livingstone, Stanley and Brazza, among others. **or**
Central Africa was explored by several Europeans, including Livingstone, Stanley and Brazza.

If you *do* find yourself using *etc.*, for heaven's sake spell it and punctuate it correctly. This is an abbreviation for the Latin phrase *et cetera* 'and other things', and it is pronounced ET SETRA, and **not** ★ EK SETRA. Do **not** write ghastly things like ★ *ect.* or ★ *e.t.c.* Such monstrosities make your writing look hopelessly illiterate. Again, if you avoid Latin abbreviations, you won't fall into such traps.

Finally, for the two further (and highly objectionable) Latin abbreviations *ibid.* and *op. cit.* see section 10.3.

Observe that it is usual to write most Latin abbreviations in italics, but this is not strictly essential, and many people don't bother.

There has recently been a fashion in some circles for writing Latin abbreviations without full stops, and you may come across things like *ie* and *eg* in your reading. I consider this a ghastly practice, and I urge you strongly not to imitate it. (Note, however, that *et al.* has only one full stop, since *et* 'and' is a complete word in Latin.)

One final point: very many people who should know better use the Latin abbreviation *cf.*, which properly means 'compare', merely to refer to published work. It is now very common to see something like this:

> ★ The Australian language Dyirbal has a remarkable gender system; *cf.* Dixon (1972).

This is quite wrong, since the writer is not inviting the reader to *compare* Dixon's work with anything, but only to consult that work for more information. Hence the correct form is this:

The Australian language Dyirbal has a remarkable gender system; see Dixon (1972).

This widespread blunder is a signal reminder of the danger of using Latin abbreviations when you don't know what they mean. Far too many writers fall into this trap, and write *i.e.* when they mean *e.g.*, or something equally awful. If you *must* use a Latin abbreviation, make sure you're using the right one. In most circumstances, though, you are best advised to avoid these abbreviations: almost every one of them has a simple English equivalent which should usually be preferred.

Summary of abbreviations

- **Do not use an abbreviation that can easily be avoided.**
- **In an abbreviation, use full stops and capital letters in the conventional way.**
- **Do not forget to punctuate the rest of the sentence normally.**

Chapter 8

Quotation Marks

8.1 Quotation Marks and Direct Quotations

The use of **quotation marks**, also called **inverted commas**, is very slightly complicated by the fact that there are two types: **single quotes** (' ') and **double quotes** (" "). As a general rule, British usage prefers single quotes for ordinary use, but double quotes are also very common; American usage insists upon double quotes. Usage in the rest of the world varies: double quotes are preferred in Canada and Australia, and perhaps also in New Zealand, while single quotes are perhaps more usual in South Africa. As we shall see below, the use of double quotes in fact offers several advantages, and this is the usage I recommend here. You may find, however, if you are writing for publication, that your editor or publisher insists upon single quotes. If you are using a word processor, though, you may find that your printer produces single quotes which are all but invisible, in which case double quotes will make life easier for your readers.

The chief use of quotation marks is quite easy to understand: a **pair** of quotation marks encloses a **direct quotation**

– that is, a repetition of someone's exact words. Here are some examples:

> President Kennedy famously exclaimed, 'Ich bin ein Berliner!'
>
> Madonna is fond of declaring, 'I'm not ashamed of anything.'
>
> 'The only emperor,' writes Wallace Stevens, 'is the emperor of ice cream.'

Look closely at these examples. Note first that what is enclosed in quotes must be the exact words of the person being quoted. Anything which is not part of those exact words must be placed outside the quotes, even if, as in the last example, this means using two sets of quotes because the quotation has been interrupted. (The commas in the last example set off a weak interruption, as usual; their presence has nothing to do with the quotation.) And note something else which is very strange: the first comma in the last example comes *inside* the quotes, even though it is not part of the quotation. This makes no sense, and it contradicts the usual principles of punctuation, but for some reason this illogical style has become almost universal in English. I don't like it, and I would very much prefer to put that comma *outside* the quotes, where it belongs, as follows:

> 'The only emperor', writes Wallace Stevens, 'is the emperor of ice cream.'

But, if you do this, you will find most of the world lined up against you. See below for more on this topic.

Otherwise, however, you should not put quotes around anything other than a word-for-word quotation. Consequently, the following example is **wrong**:

> ★ Thomas Edison declared that 'Genius was one per cent inspiration and ninety-nine per cent perspiration.'

Here the passage inside the quotes transparently does not reproduce Edison's exact words. There are three ways of fixing this. First, drop the quotes:

> Thomas Edison declared that genius was one per cent inspiration and ninety-nine per cent perspiration.

Second, rewrite the sentence so that you can use Edison's exact words:

> According to Thomas Edison, 'Genius is one per cent inspiration and ninety-nine per cent perspiration.'

Third, move the quotes so that they enclose only Edison's exact words:

> Thomas Edison declared that genius was 'one per cent inspiration and ninety-nine per cent perspiration'.

All three of these are perfect, since only Edison's exact words are enclosed in quotes.

Now notice something else which is very important: a quotation is set off by quotation marks **and nothing else**. A sentence containing a quotation is punctuated exactly like any other sentence apart from the addition of the quotation marks. You should **not** insert additional punctuation marks into the sentence merely to warn the reader that a quotation is coming up: that's what the quotation marks are for. Here are some common mistakes:

> * President Nixon declared: 'I am not a crook.'
> * President Nixon declared:– 'I am not a crook.'

The colon in the first is completely pointless, while the startling arsenal of punctuation in the second is grotesque. (Remember, a colon can never be followed by a hyphen or a dash.) Here is the style I recommend:

> President Nixon declared 'I am not a crook.'

Adding more dots and squiggles to this perfectly clear sentence would do absolutely nothing to improve it. No punctuation mark should be used if it is not necessary.

Nevertheless, very many people prefer to put a comma before an opening quote, as follows:

> President Nixon declared, 'I am not a crook.'

I consider such commas to be unnecessary, since they do no work at all, but most publishers insist upon them. If you are writing for publication, then, you will probably find yourself obliged to use them.

On the other hand, the presence of quotation marks does not remove the necessity of using other punctuation which is required for independent reasons. Look again at these examples:

> According to Thomas Edison, 'Genius is one per cent inspiration and ninety-nine per cent perspiration.'
>
> 'The only emperor,' writes Wallace Stevens, 'is the emperor of ice cream.'

The commas here are bracketing commas, used as usual to set off weak interruptions; their presence has nothing to do with the presence of a quotation, which is itself properly marked off by the quotation marks.

Here is another example:

> Mae West had one golden rule for handling men: 'Tell the pretty ones they're smart, and tell the smart ones they're pretty.'

The colon here is **not** being used merely because a quotation follows. Instead, it is doing what colons always do: it is introducing an explanation of what comes before the colon. It is merely a coincidence that what follows the colon happens to be a quotation.

This last example illustrates another point about quotations: the quotation inside the quote marks begins with a capital letter if it is a complete sentence, but not otherwise. Look once more at two versions of the Edison sentence:

> According to Thomas Edison, 'Genius is one per cent inspiration and ninety-nine per cent perspiration.'

> Thomas Edison declared that genius was 'one per cent inspiration and ninety-nine per cent perspiration'.

The first quotation is a complete sentence and therefore gets an initial capital letter; the second is not a complete sentence and hence receives no capital.

There is one situation in which the use of single quotes instead of double quotes can be rather a nuisance. This is when the quotation contains an apostrophe, especially near the end:

> Professor Cavendish concludes that 'The Turks' influence on the Balkans has been more enduring than the Greeks' ever was.'

Since an apostrophe is usually indistinguishable from a closing quote mark, the reader may be momentarily misled into thinking that she has come to the end of the quotation when she has not. This is one reason why I personally prefer to use double quotes:

> Professor Cavendish concludes that "The Turks' influence on the Balkans has been more enduring than the Greeks' ever was."

With double quotes, the problem goes away.

Things can get a little complicated when you cite a quotation that has another quotation inside it. In this rare circumstance, the rule is to set off the internal quotation with the *other* type of quotation marks. So, if you're using double quotes:

> The Shadow Employment Secretary declared,
> "Describing the unemployment figures as
> 'disappointing' is an insult to the British people."

And if you're using single quotes:

> The Shadow Employment Secretary declared,
> 'Describing the unemployment figures as
> "disappointing" is an insult to the British people.'

Naturally, you'll be asking what you should do if you have a quotation inside a quotation inside a quotation. My answer: you should rewrite the sentence. Otherwise, you will simply lose your reader in a labyrinth of quotation marks.

If you have a long quotation which you want to display indented in the middle of the page, you do not need to place quotes around it, though you should make sure that you identify it explicitly as a quotation in your main text. Here is an example cited from G. V. Carey's famous book on punctuation, *Mind the Stop* (Carey 1958):

> I should define punctuation as being governed two-thirds by rule and one-third by personal taste. I shall endeavour not to stress the former to the exclusion of the latter, but I will not knuckle under to those who apparently claim for themselves complete freedom to do what they please in the matter.

It would not be wrong to enclose this passage in quotes, but there is no need, since I have clearly identified it as a quotation, which is exactly what quotation marks normally do. No punctuation should be used if it's not doing any work.

Occasionally you may find it necessary to interrupt a quotation you are citing in order to clarify something. To do this you enclose your remarks in **square brackets** (never parentheses). Suppose I want to cite a famous passage from the eighteenth-century French writer Alexis de Tocqueville:

> These two nations [America and Russia] seem set to sway the destinies of half the globe.

The passage from which this sentence is taken had earlier made it clear which two nations the author was talking about. My quotation, however, does not make this clear, and so I have inserted the necessary information enclosed in square brackets.

Some authors, when doing this, have a habit of inserting their own initials within the square brackets, preceded by a dash. Thus, my example might have looked like this:

> These two nations [America and Russia – RLT] seem set to sway the destinies of half the globe.

This is not wrong, but it is hardly ever necessary, since the square brackets already make it clear what's going on.

There is one special interruption whose use you should be familiar with. This happens when the passage you are quoting contains a mistake of some kind, and you want to make it clear to your reader that the mistake is contained in the original passage, and has not been introduced by you. To do this, you use the Latin word *sic*, which means 'thus', again enclosed in square brackets and immediately following the mistake. The mistake can be of any kind: a spelling mistake, a grammatical error, the use of the wrong word, or even a statement which is obviously wrong or silly. Here are some examples, all of which are meant to be direct quotations:

> We have not recieved [*sic*] your letter.
> The number of students are [*sic*] larger than usual.
> The All Blacks won the match with a fortuitous [*sic*] try in the final minute.
> The last dinosaurs died about 60,000 years ago [*sic*].

(The word *received* is misspelled; the form *are* has been used where *is* is required; the word *fortuitous*, which means 'accidental', has been used where *fortunate* was intended; the last statement is grotesquely false.) Note that the word *sic* is commonly italicized, if italics are available. And note also that *sic* is **not** used merely to emphasize part of a quotation: it is used only to draw attention to an error.

If you *do* want to emphasize part of a quotation, you do so by placing that part in italics, but you must show that you are doing this. Here is a sentence cited from Steven Pinker's book *The Language Instinct*:

> Many prescriptive rules of grammar are *just plain dumb* and should be deleted from the usage handbooks [emphasis added].

Here my comment in square brackets shows that the italics were not present in the original but that I have added them in order to draw attention to this part of the quotation. In Chapter 9 we shall consider the use of italics further.

If you want to quote parts of a passage while leaving out some intervening bits, you do this by inserting an **ellipsis** (. . .) (also called a **suspension** or **omission marks**) to represent a missing section of a quotation. If, as a result, you need to provide one or two extra words to link up the pieces of the quotation, you put those extra words inside square brackets to show that they are not part of the quotation. If you need to change a small letter to a capital, you put that capital inside square brackets. Here is an example, cited from my own book *Language: The Basics* (Trask 1995):

> Chelsea was born nearly deaf, but . . . she was disastrously misdiagnosed as mentally retarded when she failed to learn to speak . . . [S]he was raised by a loving family . . . [but] only when she was thirty-one did a disbelieving doctor . . . prescribe for her a hearing aid. Able to hear speech at last, she began learning English.

Naturally, when you use an ellipsis, be careful not to misrepresent the sense of the original passage.

Finally, there remains the problem of whether to put other punctuation marks inside or outside the quotation marks. There are at least two schools of thought on this, which I shall call the *logical view* and the *conventional view*. American usage adheres closely to the conventional view; British usage prefers the logical view, but, as we shall see, with one curious exception.

The logical view holds that the only punctuation marks which should be placed inside the quotation marks are those that form part of the quotation, while all others should be placed outside. The conventional view, in contrast, insists on placing most other punctuation marks inside a closing quote, regardless of whether they form part of the quotation. Here are three sentences punctuated according to the logical view; the second is taken from Pullum (1984), of which more below:

'The only thing we have to fear', said Franklin Roosevelt, 'is fear itself.'
Bolinger never said 'Accent is predictable'; he said 'Accent is predictable – if you're a mind-reader.'
The Prime Minister condemned what he called 'simple-minded solutions'.

And here they are punctuated according to the conventional view:

'The only thing we have to fear,' said Franklin Roosevelt, 'is fear itself.'
Bolinger never said, 'Accent is predictable;' he said, 'Accent is predictable – if you're a mind-reader.'
The Prime Minister condemned what he called 'simple-minded solutions.'

Note the placing of the comma after *fear* in the first example, of the semicolon after *predictable* in the second, and of the final full stop in the third. These are not part of their quotations, and so the logical view places them outside the quote marks, while the conventional view places them inside, on the theory that a closing quote should always follow another punctuation mark.

Which view should we prefer? I certainly prefer the logical view, and, in a perfect world, I would simply advise you to stick to this view. However, it is a fact that American usage clings grimly to the conventional view, and you will find it very difficult to persuade an American publisher to refrain from changing your logical punctuation. British usage, in contrast, generally prefers the logical view, but with one inconsistent and bizarre exception: British publishers normally insist on putting a comma inside closing quotes, even when it logically belongs outside. Hence a British publisher will usually insist on the conventional style with my Roosevelt example above, but on the logical style with the other two. This is mysterious, but it's a fact of life.

The linguist Geoff Pullum, a fervent advocate of the logical view, once got so angry at copy-editors who insisted on reshuffling his carefully placed punctuation that he wrote an article called 'Punctuation and human freedom' (Pullum 1984). Here is one of his examples, first with logical punctuation, as it would usually be printed in Britain:

> Shakespeare's play *Richard III* contains the line 'Now is the winter of our discontent'.

This is true. Now try it with conventional punctuation, as preferred in the USA:

> Shakespeare's play *Richard III* contains the line 'Now is the winter of our discontent.' (A)

This is strictly false, since the line in question is only the first of two lines making up a complete sentence, and hence does not end in a full stop, as apparently suggested by the conventional punctuation:

> Now is the winter of our discontent
> Made glorious summer by this sun of York.

The same point arises in the General Sedgwick example cited in Chapter 6:

> General Sedgwick's last words to his worried staff were 'Don't worry, boys; they couldn't hit an elephant at this dist–'.

Here, putting the full stop inside the closing quotes, as required by the conventionalists, would produce an idiotic result, since the whole point of the quotation is that the lamented general didn't live long enough to finish it.

You may follow your own preference in this matter, so long as you are consistent. If you opt for logical punctuation, you will have the satisfaction of knowing that you are on the side of the angels, but you should also expect some grim opposition from the other side.

8.2 Scare Quotes

The use of quotation marks can be extended to cases which are not exactly direct quotations. Here is an example:

> Linguists sometimes employ a technique they call 'inverted reconstruction'.

The phrase in quote marks is not a quotation from anyone in particular, but merely a term which is used by some people – in this case, linguists. What the writer is doing here is *distancing* himself from the term in quotes. That is, he's saying, 'Look, that's what they call it. I'm not responsible for this term.' In this case, there is no suggestion that the writer disapproves of the phrase in quotes, but very often there *is* a suggestion of disapproval:

> The Institute for Personal Knowledge is now offering a course in 'self-awareness exercises'.

Once again, the writer's quotes mean 'this is *their* term, not mine', but this time there is definitely a hint of a sneer: the writer is implying that, although the Institute may *call* their course 'self-awareness exercises', what they're really offering to do is to take your money in exchange for a lot of hot air.

Quotation marks used in this way are informally called **scare quotes**. Scare quotes are quotation marks placed around a word or phrase from which you, the writer, wish to distance yourself because you consider that word or phrase to be odd or inappropriate for some reason. Possibly you regard it as too colloquial for formal writing; possibly you think it's unfamiliar or mysterious; possibly you consider it to be inaccurate or misleading; possibly you believe it's just plain wrong. Quite often scare quotes are used to express irony or sarcasm:

> The Serbs are closing in on the 'safe haven' of Goražde.

The point here is that the town has been officially declared a safe haven by the UN, whereas in fact, as the quote marks make clear, it is anything but safe. Here's another example:

> Sharon made dozens of 'adult films' before getting her Hollywood break.

The phrase 'adult films' is the industry's conventional label for pornographic films, and here the writer is showing that she recognizes this phrase as nothing more than a dishonest euphemism.

It is important to realize this distancing effect of scare quotes. Quotation marks are **not** properly used merely in order to draw attention to words, and all those pubs which declare *We Sell 'Traditional Pub Food'* are unwittingly suggesting to a literate reader that they are in fact serving up microwaved sludge.

Some writers perhaps take the use of scare quotes a little too far:

> I have just been 'ripped off' by my insurance company.

Here the writer is doing something rather odd: she is using the phrase ‘ripped off’, but at the same time she is showing her distaste for this phrase by wrapping it in quotes. Perhaps she regards it as too slangy, or as too American. Using scare quotes like this is the orthographic equivalent of holding the phrase at arm’s length with one hand and pinching your nose with the other.

I can’t really approve of scare quotes used in this way. If you think a word is appropriate, then use it, without any quotes; if you think it’s not appropriate, then don’t use it, unless you specifically want to be ironic. Simultaneously using a word and showing that you don’t approve of it will only make you sound like an antiquated fuddy-duddy.

8.3 Quotation Marks in Titles

A couple of generations ago, it was the custom to enclose all titles in quotation marks: titles of books, titles of poems, titles of films, titles of newspapers, and so on. This usage, however, has now largely disappeared, and the modern custom is to write most titles in italics, as explained in Chapter 9. But in academic circles, at least, it is still usual to enclose the titles of articles in journals and magazines in quotes, as well as the titles of chapters in books – hence my reference above to Geoff Pullum’s article ‘Punctuation and human freedom’. In British usage, however, we **always** use single quotes for this purpose, though American usage usually prefers double quotes here too.

It is still not exactly wrong to refer to a newspaper as 'The Guardian', or to a book as 'Uncle Tom's Cabin', but it is certainly old-fashioned now, and my advice is to use italics rather than quotation marks, except perhaps when you are writing by hand.

8.4 Talking About Words

There is one very special use of quotation marks which it is useful to know about: we use quotation marks when we are talking about words. In this special use, all varieties of English normally use only single quotes, and not double quotes (though some Americans use double quotes even here). (This is another advantage of using double quotes for ordinary purposes, since this special use can then be readily distinguished.) Consider the following examples:

Men are physically stronger than women.
'Men' is an irregular plural.

In the first example, we are using the word 'men' in the ordinary way, to refer to male human beings. In the second, however, we are doing something very different: we are not talking about any human beings at all, but instead we are talking about the *word* 'men'. Placing quotes around the word we are talking about makes this clear. Of course, you are only likely to need this device when you are writing about language, but then you should certainly use it. If you think

I'm being unnecessarily finicky, take a look at a sample of the sort of thing I frequently find myself trying to read when marking my students' essays:

> * A typical young speaker in Reading has done, not did, and usually also does for do and dos for does.

I'm sure you'll agree this is a whole lot easier to read with some suitable quotation marks:

> A typical young speaker in Reading has 'done', not 'did', and usually also 'does' for 'do' and 'dos' for 'does'.

Failure to make this useful orthographic distinction can, in rare cases, lead to absurdity:

> The word processor came into use around 1910.
> The word 'processor' came into use around 1910.

If what you mean is the second, writing the first will create momentary havoc in your reader's mind. (The second statement is true; the first is wrong by about seventy years.) Here we have a particularly clear example of the way in which good punctuation works: in speech, the phrases *the word processor* and *the word 'processor'* sound quite different, because they are stressed differently; in writing, the stress difference is lost, and punctuation must step in to do the job.

Printed books usually use italics for citing words, rather than quotation marks. If you are using a keyboard which can produce italics, you can use italics in this way, and indeed this practice is preferable to the use of quotes. See Chapter 9 for more on this. In one circumstance, though, italics are not possible: when we are providing brief translations (or *glosses*, as they are called) for *foreign* words. Here's an example:

> The English word 'thermometer' is derived from the Greek words *thermos* 'heat' and *metron* 'measure'.

This example shows the standard way of mentioning foreign words: the foreign word is put into italics, and an English translation, if provided, follows in single quotes, with **no other punctuation**. Observe that neither a comma nor anything else separates the foreign word from the gloss.

You can even do this with English words:

> The words *stationary* 'not moving' and *stationery* 'writing materials' should be carefully distinguished.

In this case, it is clearly necessary to use italics for citing English words, reserving the single quotes for the glosses.

Summary of quotation marks

- **Put quotation marks (single or double) around the exact words of a direct quotation.**
- **Inside a quotation, use a suspension to mark omitted material and square brackets to mark inserted material.**
- **Use quotation marks to distance yourself from a word or phrase or to show that you are using it ironically.**
- **Place quotation marks around a word or phrase which you are talking about.**

Chapter 9

Miscellaneous

9.1 Italics

Most word processors can produce **italics**, which are slanted letters – *like these*. If you can't produce italics, the conventional substitute is to use underlining – <u>like this</u>. Italics have several uses.

Most commonly, italics are used for emphasis or contrast – that is, to draw attention to some particular part of a text. Here are some examples:

The Battle of New Orleans was fought in January 1815, two weeks *after* the peace treaty had been signed.

According to the linguist Steven Pinker, 'Many prescriptive rules of grammar are *just plain dumb* and should be deleted from the usage handbooks' [emphasis added].

Standard English usage requires '*in*sensitive' rather than '*un*sensitive'.

Lemmings have, not two, but *three* kinds of sex chromosome.

The first two examples illustrate emphasis and the last two illustrate contrast. This is the standard way of representing emphasis or contrast; you should not try to use quotation marks or other punctuation marks for this purpose.

Another use of italics, as explained in Chapter 8, is to cite titles of complete works: books, films, journals, musical compositions, and so on:

> We saw a performance of the *Messiah* on Saturday.
> Chomsky's book *Syntactic Structures* revolutionized linguistics.
> Spielberg won his Oscars for *Schindler's List*.

An exception: the names of holy books are usually *not* written in italics. Thus, we write about the (Holy) Bible and the (Holy) Koran, with no italics. Don't ask me why.

Note, however, that we do not use italics when citing a name which is only a conventional description:

> Dvořák's ninth symphony is commonly known as the *New World* symphony.

Here the label 'Dvořák's ninth symphony' is not strictly a title, and hence is not italicized.

A third use of italics is to cite foreign words when talking about them. Examples:

> The French word *pathétique* is usually best translated as 'moving', not as 'pathetic'.
> The German word *Gemütlichkeit* is not easy to translate into English.

The Sicilian tradition of *omertà* has long protected the Mafia.

At Basque festivals, a favourite entertainment is the *sokamuturra*, in which people run in front of a bull which is restricted by ropes controlled by handlers.

Related to this is the use of italics when using foreign words and phrases which are not regarded as completely assimilated into English:

Psychologists are interested in the phenomenon of *déjà vu*.

This analysis is not in accord with the *Sprachgefühl* of native speakers.

If you are not sure which foreign words and phrases are usually written in italics, consult a good dictionary.

As explained in Chapter 8, it is also quite common to use italics when citing English words that are being talked about, as an alternative to single quotes:

The origin of the word *boy* is unknown.

Note the spelling difference between *premier* (an adjective meaning 'first' or 'most important') and *premiere* (a noun meaning 'first performance').

Finally, italics are used in certain disciplines for various specific purposes. Here are two of the commoner ones. In biology, genus and species names of living creatures are italicized:

The earliest known member of the genus *Homo* is *H. habilis*.

The cedar waxwing (*Bombycilla cedrorum*) is a familiar American bird.

Note that a genus name always has a capital letter, while a species name never does.

Second, names of legal cases are italicized:

The famous case of *Brown* v. *Board of Education* was a landmark in American legal history.

In this case, note that the abbreviation *v.*, which stands for *versus* ('against') stands in roman type, not in italics. Note also that the American abbreviation is *vs.*:

(A) The famous case of *Brown* vs. *Board of Education* was a landmark in American legal history.

Special note: If you have a sentence containing a phrase which would normally go into italics, and if for some reason the entire sentence needs to be italicized, then the phrase that would normally be in italics goes into ordinary roman type instead. So, if for some reason my last example sentence needs to be italicized, the result looks like this:

The famous case of Brown *v.* Board of Education *was a landmark in American legal history.*

9.2 Boldface

Boldface letters are the extra-black ones – **like these**. Most word processors can produce these. They have only a few general uses.

First, they are used for chapter titles and section headings, exactly as is done in this book.

Second, they are used for the captions to illustrations, tables and graphs.

Third, they are sometimes used to provide very strong emphasis, as an alternative to italics. In this book I have used them in this way very frequently – probably too frequently:

A colon is **never** followed by a hyphen or a dash.

Finally, boldface is often used to introduce important new terms. Again, I have been doing this regularly in this book: the name of each new punctuation mark is introduced in boldface.

The judicious use of boldface can provide variety and make a page more attractive to the eye, but it is never essential. If you can't produce boldface, use ordinary roman type for chapter and section headings and captions, and italics for emphasis and important terms. If you do use boldface, don't overdo it.

9.3 Small Capitals

Small capitals are just what they sound like: THEY LOOK LIKE THIS. They have only one common use: certain abbreviations are commonly written in small capitals. In particular, the abbreviations BC and AD are usually so written:

> Alexander the Great died in 323 BC.
> Charlemagne was crowned in Rome on Christmas Day, AD 800.

Recall too that American usage prefers to write the time of day with small capitals:

> (A) The earthquake struck at 6:40 AM.

In British usage, this would appear as follows:

> The earthquake struck at 6.40 a.m.

A few publishers have recently adopted the practice of putting *all* abbreviations in small capitals, but this is not something you should imitate.

Many word processors can produce small capitals; if you can't produce them, use full capitals instead:

> Alexander the Great died in 323 BC.

Very occasionally, small capitals are used for emphasis, but it is usually preferable to use italics for this, or even boldface.

9.4 Parentheses

Parentheses (( )), also called **round brackets**, always occur in pairs. They have one major use and one or two minor uses.

Most commonly, a pair of parentheses is used to set off a strong or weak interruption, rather like a pair of dashes or a pair of bracketing commas. In the case of a strong interruption, very often it is possible to use either dashes or parentheses:

> The destruction of Guernica – and there is no doubt that the destruction was deliberate – horrified the world.
> The destruction of Guernica (and there is no doubt that the destruction was deliberate) horrified the world.

As a rule, however, we prefer parentheses, rather than dashes or bracketing commas, when the interruption is best regarded as a kind of 'aside' from the writer to the reader:

> On the (rare!) occasion when you use a Latin abbreviation, be sure to punctuate it correctly.
> The battle of Jutland (as you may recall from your school days) put an end to Germany's naval threat.
> The Basque language is not (as the old legend has it) exceedingly difficult to learn.

We also use parentheses to set off an interruption which merely provides additional information or a brief explanation of an unfamiliar term:

The number of living languages (currently about 6000, by most estimates) is decreasing rapidly.
The *bodegas* (wine cellars) of the Rioja are an essential stop on any visit to northern Spain.
The royal portraits of Velázquez (or Velásquez) are justly renowned.
The German philosopher Gottlob Frege (1848–1925) laid the foundations of formal logic and of semantics.

In the last two examples, the phrases in parentheses merely provide an alternative spelling of the painter's name and the birth and death dates of the philosopher. In all these examples, neither dashes nor bracketing commas would be possible, except that you might conceivably use dashes in the first. Note also the way I introduce each new punctuation mark in this book.

It is possible to put an entire sentence into parentheses, or even a series of sentences, if they constitute an interruption of an appropriate type:

It appears that 33% of girls aged 16–18 smoke regularly, but that only 28% of boys in this age bracket do so. (These figures are provided by a recent newspaper survey.)

Note that a sentence in parentheses is capitalized and punctuated in the normal fashion.

Do not overdo parentheses to the point of stuffing one entire sentence inside another:

* The first-ever international cricket match (very few cricket fans are aware of this) was played between Canada and the United States in 1844.

This sort of thing is very common in the writing of those who neither plan their sentences ahead nor polish their writing afterward. If you find you have done this, rewrite the sentence in some less overcrowded way:

Very few cricket fans are aware that the first-ever international cricket match was played between Canada and the United States in 1844. **or**
The first-ever international cricket match was played between Canada and the United States in 1844. Very few cricket fans are aware of this.

Parentheses may also be used to represent options:

The referees who decide whether an abstract should be accepted will not know the name(s) of the author(s).
The (french) horn is an unusually difficult instrument to play.

The point of the last example is that the names *french horn* and *horn* denote the same instrument.

Finally, parentheses are used to enclose numerals or letters in an enumeration included in the body of a text:

A book proposal prepared for a potential publisher should include at least (1) a description of the content, (2) an identification of the intended readership, (3) an explanation of why the book will be necessary or valuable and (4) a comparison with any competing books already in print.

Observe that, in contrast to what happens with dashes and bracketing commas, we **always** write both parentheses:

He was smitten by a *coup de foudre* (as the French none too romantically put it).

Occasionally you may find yourself placing one set of parentheses inside another. Sometimes this is unavoidable, but you should avoid it whenever possible, since it makes your sentence hard to follow.

9.5 Square Brackets

There is only one common use for **square brackets** ([ ]). As was explained in Chapter 8, square brackets are used to set off an interruption within a direct quotation; refer to that chapter for details.

Very occasionally square brackets are used for citing references; see Chapter 10.

Specialist fields like mathematics and linguistics use square brackets for certain purposes of their own, but these are beyond the scope of this book.

9.6 The Ellipsis

The **ellipsis** (. . .), also called the **suspension** or **omission marks**, has just two uses.

First, as was explained in Chapter 8, the ellipsis is used to show that some material has been omitted from the middle of a direct quotation; see that chapter for details.

Second, the ellipsis is used to show that a sentence has been left unfinished. Unlike the dash, which is used to show that an utterance has been broken off abruptly (recall the unfortunate General Sedgwick!), the suspension shows that the writer or speaker has simply 'tailed off' into silence, deliberately leaving something unsaid:

> Colonel García leered at the prisoner: 'We want those names now. If we don't get them . . .'
>
> San Francisco gets a major earthquake about every sixty years. It has been ninety years since the last one . . .

This second usage is more typical of journalistic prose than of formal writing; excepting only when you are citing a direct quotation which seems to require it, you should generally avoid the ellipsis in formal writing.

9.7 The Slash

The **slash** (/), also called the **oblique**, the **virgule**, the **stroke**, the **solidus** or the **shilling mark**, has several uses, all of them rather minor.

First, it is used to separate alternatives:

> Applicants must possess a good university degree in French and/or have worked for two years in a French-speaking country.
>
> Each candidate must bring his/her identity card.
>
> If your work is badly punctuated, your reader may quickly decide that s/he has better things to do.

This usage is rather hard on the eye, and it is usually preferable to write the alternatives out in full:

> Each candidate must bring his or her identity card.

This style is particularly frequent in job advertisements:

> The University of Saffron Walden wishes to appoint a lecturer/senior lecturer in media studies.

Second, the slash may be used to represent a period of time:

> The 1994/95 football season was marred by frequent scandals.
>
> This office is open Tuesday/Saturday each week.

Third, the slash is used, especially in scientific writing, to represent the word *per* in units:

The density of iron is 7.87 g/cm^3.

Light travels at 300,000 km/sec.

Fourth, the slash is used in writing fractions, as in ¾ or 3/4; in this use, it is often called the **scratch**. (See the next section for usage.)

Fifth, the slash is used in writing certain abbreviations. Virtually the only one of these you will find outside of specialist contexts is *c/o* for 'care of' in addresses:

Write to me at Sylvia Keller, c/o Andrea Mason, 37 The Oaks, Plumtree, East Sussex BN17 4GH.

Finally, slashes are used to separate lines of poetry when a poem is written solid, instead of being set out line by line:

When you are old and grey and full of sleep/And nodding by the fire, take down this book/And slowly read of the soft look/Your eyes had once, and of their shadows deep. (W. B. Yeats)

9.8 Numerals, Fractions and Dates

The compound numerals from twenty-one to ninety-nine are written with hyphens:

France is divided into ninety-six departments.

Mozart was only thirty-five years old when he died.

No additional hyphens are used in writing larger numbers:

A leap year has three hundred and sixty-six days.

The maximum possible score with three darts is one hundred and eighty.

In formal writing, the numerals from one to twenty are almost always written out:

The American flag has thirteen stripes.

We have four candidates for president.

Do **not** write:

* The American flag has 13 stripes.

* We have 4 candidates for president.

Larger numbers, however, may be written with digits, if you prefer:

The bomb killed 37 people and injured over 200 others.

Writing was invented less than 6000 years ago.

It is, however, always acceptable to write out numbers up to ninety-nine, and in fact some publishers will insist upon this; if you are writing for publication, you should check:

The bomb killed thirty-seven people and injured over 200 others.

When writing a four-digit numeral in digits (other than a date), American writers never use a comma, but British writers usually do. Hence Americans write *2000 years* and *3700 people*, while Britons often write *2,000 years* and *3,700 people.*

I consider such commas completely pointless, and I don't use them myself, but others may insist that you do so. A five-digit or larger numeral always takes one or more commas: *53,000 refugees, 170,000 cases of AIDS, 2,760,453 patents.*

Naturally, we make an exception for addresses and other special cases, in which numerals are always written with digits:

I lived for years at 4 Howitt Road in Belsize Park.

Observe that it is bad style to start a sentence with a numeral: either the number should be written out, or the sentence should be rewritten:

* 650 MPs sit in Parliament.
Six hundred and fifty MPs sit in Parliament.
There are 650 MPs in Parliament.

Fractions are always written with hyphens:

Almost three-fourths of the earth's surface is water.
More than one-half of babies born are male.

But note the following case:

One half of me wants to take the job while the other half doesn't.

Here the phrase *one half* is not really a fraction at all.

In formal writing, a fraction is always written out. You should **not** write things like the following:

★ Almost ¾ of the earth's surface is water.

In writing a date, it is increasingly common today to use no commas:

It was on 18 April 1775 that Paul Revere made his famous ride.

On December 7 1941 the Japanese attacked Pearl Harbor.

She died on the last day of November 1843.

An older style, still acceptable, puts commas around the year:

It was on 18 April, 1775, that Paul Revere made his famous ride.

On December 7, 1941, the Japanese attacked Pearl Harbor.

She died on the last day of November, 1843.

You may use either fashion, so long as you are consistent.

Important note: In British usage, a date is written day-month-year, while American usage prefers month-day-year. Hence, Britons write *23 March*, while Americans write *March 23*. This is a potentially serious problem when we use the abbreviated style of writing dates often found in letters and business documents: to a Briton, *5/7/84* means *5 July 1984*, while to an American it means *May 7 1984*. If you are writing something that might be read on the other side of the Atlantic, therefore, it is best to write out a date in full, to avoid any misunderstanding.

9.9 Diacritics

Diacritics, often loosely called 'accents', are the various little dots and squiggles which, in many languages, are written above, below or on top of certain letters of the alphabet to indicate something about their pronunciation. Thus, French has words like *été* 'summer', *août* 'August', *ça* 'that' and *père* 'father'; German has *Wörter* 'words' and *tschüss* 'good-bye'; Spanish has *mañana* 'tomorrow' and *ángel* 'angel'; Norwegian has *brød* 'bread' and *frå* 'from'; Polish has *łza* 'tear', *źle* 'badly' and *pięć* 'five'; Turkish has *kuş* 'bird' and *göz* 'eye'; Welsh has *tŷ* 'house' and *sïo* 'hiss', and so on. When you are citing a word, a name or a passage from a foreign language which uses diacritics, you should make every effort to reproduce those diacritics faithfully. Fortunately, most word processors can produce at least the commoner diacritics.

You are most likely to need to do this when citing names of persons or places or titles of literary and musical works. The French politician is *François Mitterrand*, the Spanish golfer is *José-María Olazábal*, the Polish linguist is *Jerzy Kuryłowicz*, the Turkish national hero is *Mustafa Kemal Atatürk*, the town in the former Yugoslavia is *Goražde*, Wagner's opera is the *Götterdämmerung* and the French film is *Zazie dans le Métro*. So far as you can produce them, therefore, these are the forms you should use even when writing in English. But don't overdo it. If an accepted English form exists, use that: write *Munich*, not *München*, *Montreal*, not *Montréal*, *The Magic Flute*, not *Die Zauberflöte*.

In English, diacritics are not normally used, but they occur in three situations. First, many foreign words and phrases have been borrowed into English, and some of these are not yet regarded as fully anglicized. Such forms should be written with their original diacritics, and they should also be written in italics, if possible, to show their foreign status:

Lloyd George was the Tories' *bête noire*.
She was an artist *manquée*.
The *Wörter und Sachen* approach is favoured by some etymologists.

Many other such items have become so completely anglicized that they are now usually treated as ordinary English words. Hence, most people now write *cafe*, rather than *café*, *naive*, rather than *naïve*, and *cortege*, rather than *cortège*, and such words are not normally italicized in any case. If you are in doubt about these, you should, as always, consult a good dictionary.

Second, one particular diacritic, the **diaeresis** (¨), is very occasionally written in English to show that a vowel is to be pronounced separately. A familiar example of this is the name *Zoë*, but other cases exist. A few people write *coöperate*, rather than *cooperate*, and *aërate*, rather than *aerate*, but the spellings with the diaeresis are now decidedly old-fashioned and not recommended. Usage varies with the surname *Brontë*: all the members of this famous family spelled their name with the diaeresis, which should therefore perhaps be retained by the usual rule of respecting the preferences of the owner of a name, but many people nevertheless now write *Bronte*.

Third, a **grave accent** (`) is occasionally written over the letter *e* in the ending *-ed* to show that it is pronounced as a separate syllable. Thus we write *a learnèd scholar* or *an agèd man* to show that *learnèd* and *agèd* are each pronounced here as two syllables. Compare *I learned French at school* and *He has aged rapidly*, in which *learned* and *aged* are pronounced as single syllables.

For convenience, here are the names of the commoner diacritics:

á	the **acute accent**
à	the **grave accent**
â	the **circumflex accent**
ā	the **macron**
ă	the **breve**
č	the **hachek**, or **wedge**, or **caron**
ü	the **diaeresis**, or **trema**, or **umlaut**
ñ	the **tilde**
ç	the **cedilla**
å	the **ring**, or **bolle**
ą	the **ogonek**, or **hook**
ø	the **slash**, or **solidus**, or **virgule**

9.10 The Other Marks on Your Keyboard

Your keyboard contains a number of other characters, most of which are not properly punctuation marks at all, and very few of which are normally used in formal writing, except in certain specialist disciplines. Here are the ones which are found most commonly, or which can be produced with a word processor; such special symbols are often informally called **dingbats**:

% the **per cent sign**

$ the **dollar sign**

£ the **pound sign**

¢ the **cent sign**

the **hash mark** (in computer parlance, the 'pound sign')

* the **asterisk** (in the US, informally called a 'bug')

• the **bullet**

@ the **at sign**

& the **ampersand**, or **and sign**

¶ the **paragraph mark**, or **blind**, or **pilcrow**

§ the **section mark**

|| the **parallel mark**

^ the **caret**

~ the **swung dash** (informally called the 'twiddle' or 'tilde')

_ the **underbar**

< the **less-than sign**

> the **greater-than sign**
< > **angle brackets**
{ } **braces** (also called **curly brackets**)
« » **guillemets** (French quotation marks)
» « **reversed guillemets** (German quotation marks)
+ the **plus sign**
± the **plus-or-minus sign**
= the **equal sign**
\ the **backslash**
| the **pipe**
· the **centre(d) dot**

You will undoubtedly be familiar with the use of the per cent sign, the dollar sign and the pound sign:

Over 40% of Australia is desert.
The USA bought Alaska for only $3 million.
This word processor costs £1800.

Note that we write £42.50, and **not** * £42.50p, and similarly for other currencies.

Most computer keyboards lack the pound sign, but it can usually be produced in one way or another. If you absolutely can't produce a pound sign, it has become conventional in computing circles to use the hash mark instead (hence its other name):

This word processor costs #1800.

In American English, the hash mark is used informally to represent the word 'number' before a numeral, as in *look for*

27 (A). This is not usual in British English, and it is out of place in formal writing.

The asterisk is occasionally used to mark footnotes; see Chapter 10. It also has one other rather curious use: it is sometimes used to replace a letter in writing a word which is felt to be too coarse to be written out in full, as in *f**k*. This is a usage mostly found in newspapers and magazines, in which writers are often careful to avoid offending their very broad readership. In most other types of writing, such words are normally written out in full if they are used at all. (Compare the somewhat similar use of the dash in section 6.2.)

A bullet may be used to mark each item in an enumeration if numbering of the items is not thought to be necessary; look at the summaries at the ends of most of the earlier sections of this book.

The at sign is chiefly confined to business documents, in which it stands for 'at a price of . . . each':

200 shower units @ £42.50

It is also used in electronic mail addresses to separate a username from the rest of the address, as in my e-mail address:

larryt@cogs.susx.ac.uk

The ampersand represents the word 'and' in the names of certain companies and legal firms, as in the name *Barton & Maxwell, Solicitors*. Except when citing such a name, you should **never** use an ampersand in place of 'and' in formal writing, nor should you use a plus sign for this purpose. The word 'and' is always written out.

The paragraph mark and the section mark are occasionally used to represent the words 'paragraph' and 'section' when referring to some part of a work: *in ¶ 2, in § 3.1*. They are only appropriate when brevity is important, such as in footnotes; in your text, you should write these words out: *in paragraph two, in section 3.1*.

The remaining symbols in my list have various particular uses in specialist disciplines, and sometimes in dictionaries, but they have no function in ordinary writing.

9.11 Priority Among Punctuation Marks

As I hope you have gathered by now, punctuation marks are, in most cases, independent of one another. Each mark is inserted to do a particular job, and using one mark neither allows you to drop another one which is independently required nor permits you to insert one or two extra marks which are not needed. There are, however, a few exceptions.

First of all, we never write two full stops at the end of a sentence. Observe the following examples:

> Officially, the clocks will go back at 2.00 a.m.
>
> Leo Durocher never in fact made that famous remark 'Nice guys finish last.'

The abbreviation and the direct quotation already end in full stops, so no second full stop is written. Similarly, if a sentence would logically end in two question marks, only the first is written:

Who wrote the sonnet that begins 'How do I love thee?'

If a sentence-final quotation ends in a question mark or an exclamation mark, no full stop follows:

Pontius Pilate famously asked, 'What is truth?'

However, a question mark *is* written after a full stop if this is logically required:

Does the flight arrive at 7.00 a.m. or 7.00 p.m.?

You already know that the second of two bracketing commas or dashes is not written at the end of a sentence. This is because the comma or dash that would logically appear there is 'outranked' by the full stop or other mark that appears at the end of the sentence:

The Spaniards and the Canadians are close to war over fishing rights, it would appear.
We commonly assume that there are only two sexes – but could we be wrong?

In the same way, a comma that should logically appear is suppressed if a colon or a semicolon is present at the same position:

The planet Venus is a hellhole, as the Russian probes have revealed; no human could survive for a moment on its surface.
Only two groups are excluded from the French Foreign Legion, according to the rules: women and Frenchmen.

In these examples the second bracketing commas that would logically appear after the words *revealed* and *rules* are suppressed by the following colon and semicolon. Here is a useful rule of thumb: a comma is **never** preceded or followed by any other punctuation mark at all, except possibly by a quotation mark or by a full stop which forms part of an abbreviation.

Chapter 10

Punctuating Essays and Letters

There are a few special points to be considered in writing essays, reports and articles, and in writing letters. We will consider these points in this chapter. There is in practice a good deal of variation in these matters, and the usages I recommend here are those which are common and generally acceptable. You may find, however, that your teacher, your university tutor, your business firm or your publisher insists upon some different usages from those I describe here. If so, you should, of course, conform to those requirements. Note that printed books and popular magazines sometimes depart from the normal usages in order to make their pages look attractive or eye-catching; you should leave such decisions to designers and layout editors, and not try to imitate them yourself.

10.1 Titles and Section Headings

The title of a complete work is usually centred near the top of the first page; if possible, it should be printed either in large letters or in boldface, or even in both. It should not be italicized or placed in quotation marks, and it should not have a full stop at the end. Any punctuation or italics which are required for independent reasons should be used normally; this includes a question mark at the end if the title is a question. If there is a subtitle, a colon should be placed at the end of the title proper; unless the title and the subtitle are both very short, it is best to use two lines.

There are two possible styles for capitalization: you may capitalize every significant word, or you may capitalize only those words which intrinsically require capitals, as explained in Chapter 7. (The first word should be capitalized in any case.) Here are some examples; I have used the second style of capitalization:

The origin of Mozart's *Requiem*

The imposition of English in Wales

Classroom discipline in Birmingham schools:
a case study

Football hooligans: why do they do it?

The parasites of the quaking aspen (*Populus tremuloides*)

'Thou unnecessary letter':
the history of the letter Z in English

The quotation marks in the last example are used because the first phrase is a quotation from Shakespeare.

In a work which is very short (no more than five or six pages), it is rarely necessary to divide the work into sections.

Longer works, however, are usually best divided into sections which are at least named and possibly also numbered; numbers are recommended if there are more than two or three sections. Section headings are usually placed in boldface but in ordinary-sized type; they are not centred but placed at the left-hand margin. A section heading may be placed on a separate line (with a following blank line), or it may be placed at the beginning of a paragraph; only in the second case should there be a full stop at the end. Here is an example illustrated in each of the two styles:

> **3. The dictatorship of Primo de Rivera**
>
> In 1923, King Alfonso XIII handed over power to General Primo de Rivera, who immediately abrogated the Constitution, dissolved the Cortes and installed a brutal right-wing dictatorship . . . **or**
>
> **3. The dictatorship of Primo de Rivera.** In 1923, King Alfonso XIII handed over power to General Primo de Rivera, who immediately abrogated the Constitution, dissolved the Cortes and installed a brutal right-wing dictatorship . . .

Either style is acceptable. Note that the *first* paragraph after a title or a section heading is not indented; all following paragraphs should be indented.

If the work is very long, or if it consists of a number of points and subpoints (as is often the case with bureaucratic and business documents), then the sections may be further divided into subsections. In this case, you should certainly number all the sections and subsections, in the following manner (these passages are taken from John Wells's book *Accents of English*) (Wells 1982):

6. North American English

6.1. General American

6.1.1. Introduction

In North America it is along the Atlantic coast that we find the sharpest regional and social differences in speech . . .

6.1.2. The ***thought-lot*** **merger**

A well-known diagnostic for distinguishing the northern speech area of the United States from the midland and southern areas is the pronunciation of the word *on* . . .

10.2 Footnotes

A **footnote** is a piece of text which, for some reason, cannot be accommodated within the main body of the document and which is therefore placed elsewhere. It is usual, and preferable, to place footnotes at the bottom of the page on which they are referred to, but this usually requires a great deal of fiddling about, unless you are lucky enough to have a word processor which arranges footnotes automatically. It is easier for the writer to put all the footnotes at the end of the document, but of course this makes life harder for the reader, who is obliged to do a lot of fumbling about in order to find the footnotes. **Exception**: If you are preparing a work for publication, then you must put all the footnotes on separate pages at the end of your document; such notes are called **endnotes**. But don't use endnotes in a document which will pass directly from your hands to the reader.

There are two main rules in the use of footnotes. First:

Do **not** use a footnote if you can possibly avoid it.

The overuse of footnotes will make your work laborious to read: a reader who finds herself constantly directed away from your text to consult footnotes will lose the thread of your writing and possibly lose her place altogether. The use of avoidable footnotes is self-indulgent and sloppy, and it is contemptuous of the reader. Academic writers in particular are often guilty of this kind of objectionable behaviour. Far too often I have wearily chased up a footnote only to find something like this at the end of the trail:

[7] This term is used in the sense of Halliday (1968). **or**
[23] As is commonly assumed. **or even**
[51] (1878–1941).

(The last example provides nothing but the birth and death dates of someone mentioned in the text.) Such trivial asides could easily be incorporated into the main text inside parentheses, and that's where they should be, if they're going to be present at all.

But **think** whether such information needs to be present at all. If the term being footnoted in the first of these examples is so obscure, why not merely explain it? What is your reader supposed to do if she doesn't recognize it – put your book down, go off to the library and find Halliday (1968), and read that book from cover to cover? You should make every effort to make your work a pleasure to read. Reading it should not be an epic struggle on the part of your hapless reader.

If you decide that a footnote is unavoidable, then the standard procedure is to flag it in the text with a superscript numeral at the point at which it is relevant:

> Let us consider the case of Algerian immigrants in Marseille, for whom a substantial number of case studies[6] are now available.

At the bottom of the page (one hopes), the reader will find your footnote:

> [6]I am indebted to Sylvette Vaucluse for kindly providing me with unpublished data from her own research, and to Sylvette Vaucluse and Jacqueline Labéguerie for illuminating discussions of these case studies. They are not to be held responsible for the use I make of the work here.

If you can't produce superscript numerals, then the alternative is to place the footnote numeral inside of parentheses or, preferably, square brackets:

> Let us consider the case of Algerian immigrants in Marseille, for whom a substantial number of case studies[6] are now available.

The second rule about footnotes is also a prohibition:

> Do **not** use a footnote merely to introduce a reference to work which you are citing.

The proper way to cite such references is explained in the next section.

If your footnotes are very few in number (and one hopes that they are), it is permissible to use symbols rather than numerals to flag them. The symbol most commonly used for this purpose is the **asterisk** (*):

> Let us consider the case of Algerian immigrants in Marseille, for whom a substantial number of case studies* are now available.

I do not recommend this, for two reasons. First, if you happen to be writing in a specialist field in which the asterisk is used for other purposes (as it is in mathematics and linguistics), then your reader may not immediately recognize what the asterisk is doing. Second, if you want to put more than one footnote on a page, you have a problem. Printed books sometimes trot out a startling array of further doodahs to mark additional footnotes, such as the **dagger**, or **obelisk**, or **obelus** (†) and the **double dagger**, or **diesis** (‡). Using these squiggles will at least force you to put your footnotes at the bottom of the page, but it is far better to use numerals.

A footnote should be as brief as possible, and here alone it is preferable to make liberal use of readily identifiable abbreviations, including those Latin abbreviations to which I objected so strongly in Chapter 7.

Footnotes at the bottom of the page must be set off in some way from the main text. The common way of doing this is to put the footnotes in a smaller typeface. If you can't do this, a horizontal line is permissible.

If a footnote is too long to fit at the bottom of its page, it may be continued at the bottom of the next page. When this starts to happen to you, though, you may well begin to wonder whether that footnote is really essential after all.

Don't use footnotes if you can avoid them.

10.3 References to Published Work

Especially in academic writing, it is frequently necessary to refer in your text to other work of which you have made use or to which you want to direct the reader's attention. There are several different systems for doing this, and they are not all equally good.

By far the best system is the **Harvard system**, also called the **author–date system**, and this is the one I recommend. In the Harvard system, you provide a reference in the form of the author's surname and the year of publication; this is enough to direct the reader to the list of full references in your bibliography. Like any brief interruption, the date is enclosed in parentheses, and the surname goes there too, unless it is a structural part of the sentence. Multiple references are separated by commas. Where necessary, a few words of explanation may also be placed inside the parentheses. Here are some examples:

A recent study (Barrutia 1992) has uncovered further evidence for this analysis.
Several earlier investigators (Wale 1967, Ciaramelli 1972, Mott 1974) reported just such a correlation.
These figures are cited from Curtis (1987), the most comprehensive treatment to date.
Roberts has developed this approach in a series of publications (1981, 1984, 1989).
This topic has been explored most thoroughly by Lumley (1984, 1985, 1987, 1988).
Very many investigators (for example, Scacchi 1980) have argued for the first view.

If your work includes references to two people with the same surname, use initials to distinguish them. For example, if you have both John Anderson and Stephen Anderson in your bibliography:

This approach is explored by J. Anderson (1995).

If you need to cite two or more works by the same author published in the same year, use the letters *a*, *b*, *c*, and so on, to distinguish them:

The significance of these observations is denied by several workers, including Goodlet (1990b), Shiels (1992) and White (1993a).

If you need to do this, then, of course, be sure you use the letters consistently right throughout your references and your bibliography. Finally, if you want to refer the reader to some specific pages of the work you are citing, put the page numbers after the date, with a colon intervening:

> For a description of this method, see Rogers (1978: 371–2).

Many people do not put a white space after the colon in this usage, but I prefer to do so. Some people use a comma instead of a colon, but the colon is much easier on the eye and avoids any possibility of ambiguity, so I recommend that you use a colon.

Very occasionally you may need to cite something which somebody else has told you personally, either in conversation or in a personal letter. You do it like this:

> This information has been provided by Jane Guest (personal communication).

In academic circles it is permissible to abbreviate *(personal communication)* to *(p.c.)*.

A second widely used system is the **number system**, which is particularly popular in some scientific circles. Here a reference takes the form merely of a number enclosed in square brackets:

> A recent study [17] has uncovered further evidence for this analysis.
>
> Several earlier investigators [5, 11, 23] reported just such a correlation.

This saves space, but it has several drawbacks: it gives the reader no clue as to what work is being cited, it obliges you to number all the items in your bibliography, it makes the citing of page numbers slightly awkward and it forces you to cite an author's name when that name is part of your sentence but to leave the name out otherwise. I don't like this system, and I don't recommend it, but you may at times find yourself obliged to use it.

There are several other ways of citing references, but they are all highly objectionable and should never be used. A few writers put complete references into the body of the text, which is both distracting to the reader and absurdly inefficient, especially when the same work is cited several times. Very many writers have the bad habit of putting references into footnotes and flagging them just like ordinary footnotes; not only does this practice clutter the page with pointless footnotes, but it wastes the reader's time by constantly sending her off to consult 'footnotes' which are nothing but references. Do **not** use footnotes for references.

Worst of all is the dreadful hotchpotch used by many scholars in arts subjects, in which references are presented sometimes in footnotes and sometimes in the text and are almost always incomplete and full of cryptic abbreviations which the reader has no hope of deciphering. If you spatter your work with unexplained exotica like *DCELC*, *REW* 1317, *Schuch. Prim.*, *Urquijo BSP IV, 137 ff.*, and so on, then no doubt the other eighteen specialists in your field will follow you, all right, but the rest of your readers will be helpless. Do **not** provide incomplete references, and do **not** use unexplained abbreviations. If you find that the use of some abbreviation is unavoidable, then explain it clearly, either the first time you use it, or, better still, in a list of abbreviations at the *beginning* of your work.

The perpetrators of such inexcusable obscurity have the further outrageous habit of citing references with the Latin abbreviations *ibid.* and *op. cit.* What do these mean? Well, *ibid.* means 'This is another reference to the last thing I cited; it's back there somewhere, maybe only a page or two, if you're lucky.' And *op. cit.* means 'This is another reference to the work by this author which I cited some time ago, and, if you want to know what it is, you can leaf back through twenty-five or fifty pages to find it, you miserable peasant.' (Technically, they mean 'in the same place' and 'in the work cited', but my explanations are far more honest.) **Don't use these ghastly things.** A writer who uses them is expressing utter contempt for the reader, and should be turned over to the Imperial Chinese Torturer for corrective treatment.

Use the Harvard system. It's vastly superior to everything else.

10.4 Bibliography

In any piece of written work in which you have cited references to published works, it is necessary to provide a **bibliography**, or list of references, at the end of your work.

You should provide only **one** such list. For some reason,

many people have acquired the curious belief that they should give *two* lists: one list of all the references in the order they occur, and a second alphabetical list, or something similar. This silly practice is a pointless waste of time and paper: there should be only one list of references, and the references in your text should direct the reader straight to that list, as explained in section 10.3 above.

The precise form of your bibliography may vary slightly, depending on what system you have used for citing references in your document. Here I shall assume that you have used the Harvard system, as recommended.

The bibliography is put into alphabetical order according to the surnames of the authors and editors you are citing. If you cite two authors with the same surname, put them in alphabetical order by their first names or initials. If you cite several different works by the same author, put them in date order, earliest to latest. If you have two or more works with the same author and the same date, use the *a*, *b*, *c* system described in the last section. When you cite multiple works by the same author, that author's name need be written out only once; for succeeding works, you can use an extra-long dash instead of repeating the name. A book with no author or editor is listed alphabetically by its title.

There are just three types of work which are very commonly cited in bibliographies: books, articles in books, and articles in journals. For each type, the form of the reference is slightly different, but, above all, the reference must be **complete**.

For a book, you must give the name(s) of the author(s) or editor(s), the date, the title, the place of publication and the name of the publisher. For an article in a book, you must give the name(s) of the author(s), the title of the article and the first and last pages, as well as full information on the book itself, as just described. For an article in a journal, you must give the name(s) of the author(s), the date, the title of the article, the name of the journal, the volume number and the first and last pages. Names of authors should be given just as they appear in their publications.

If you are citing two or more articles from a single book, you can put that book into your list as usual, and cross-refer each article to that book, as shown below.

There are several slightly different systems for arranging and punctuating references in a bibliography, almost all of them acceptable. They differ chiefly in whether they use full stops or commas to separate parts of the reference, in whether they put quotation marks around the titles of articles, and in where they place the date. I recommend full stops rather than commas, single quotation marks around titles of articles, and the placing of the date immediately after the author's name, and that is the system used in my examples below. Standard sources like *The MLA Style Guide* often recommend slightly different systems, and your tutor or publisher may insist upon one of these; in that case, you should fall into line, but make sure your references are complete.

Here is a sample bibliography; note that each item is

presented with what is called a 'hanging indent' (every line indented except the first):

Anderson, Henrietta. 1986. *A Study of Shoes*. New York: Cavalier Press.

— 1989a. *American Footwear: A Cultural History*. Boston: Institute for American Cultural Studies.

— 1989b. *The Rise and Rise of the Stiletto Heel*. New York: Cavalier Press.

Cannon, Felix (ed.). 1964. *European Footwear: A Collection of Readings*. Oxford: John Compton & Sons.

Ginsberg, Sylvie and Kate Bruton (eds). 1977. *If the Shoe Fits: Essays on the History of Footwear*. San Diego: Malibu Press.

Halliwell, C. N. 1990. 'The Irish brogue'. In C. L. James and P. T. Caldwell (eds). *British and Irish Footwear 1720–1880*. Dublin: Irish Academy of Arts. Pp. 173–203.

Institute for American Cultural Studies. 1978. *A Sourcebook on American Costume*. Boston: Institute for American Cultural Studies.

Jensen, Carla. 1964. 'The wellington boot'. In Cannon (1964), pp. 358–71.

Kaplan, Irene. 1983. 'The evolution of the stiletto heel'. *American Journal of Costume* 17: 38–51.

— 1990a. Review of Anderson (1989b). *American Journal of Costume* 24: 118–121.

— 1990b. 'The platform shoe and its influence'. *Boots and Shoes* 23: 154–178.

Maxwell, Catherine. 1982. 'The ski boot: practical footwear or fashion accessory?' *Boots and Shoes* 15: 1–37.

Maxwell, Catherine and Henrietta Anderson. 1981. 'The great American sneaker'. *Boots and Shoes* 14: 77–92.

Maxwell, George. 1964. 'Italian Renaissance footwear'. In Cannon (1964), pp. 105–138.

Shoes and Boots: A Compendium. 1950. London: British Museum.

Note carefully how these references are given. If you need to cite some other kind of work, such as a newspaper article, a sound recording, a film, a video, a radio or television broadcast or a CD-ROM, you should consult a comprehensive source such as *The MLA Style Manual.* However, so long as your reference is complete, you can't go too far wrong.

One further point. If you have to enter a title in your alphabetical list, ignore the words *the*, *a* and *an* at the beginning. So, a book entitled *A History of Footwear* would be listed under H, not under A, and the newspaper called *The New York Times* would be listed under N, not T.

If you are using the number system for citing references, then, of course, each item in your bibliography must be preceded by its number. You should still, however, put those items in alphabetical order. Many people who use the number system simply list the items in the order in which they occur in the text. This allows the reader to find a particular reference, all right, but she can no longer glance at your bibliography to see if particular authors or works are present. All readers will find this unhelpful, at best, and a university tutor is likely to be very annoyed.

10.5 Paragraphing

It is beyond the scope of this book to treat paragraphing in detail. Here I content myself with a few brief remarks.

Every piece of written work should be broken up into a series of reasonably small paragraphs, and each new paragraph should represent some kind of break, however small, in the continuity of the text. Some people have trouble with this, and tend to produce enormous paragraphs running to a whole page or more. This is very tiring for the reader and should be avoided. If you have this kind of problem, try studying the paragraphs in any longish section of this book; this may help you to get a grasp of where it is appropriate to start a new paragraph.

As remarked above, the first paragraph after a title or a section heading is not indented (again, look at the paragraphs in this book). Every succeeding paragraph should be indented; the tab key on any keyboard will do this for you.

For certain kinds of writing, such as technical reports and business letters, there is another format which is sometimes preferred. In this second format, every paragraph is separated from the next by a blank line, and no paragraphs are indented. This format uses more paper, and it is not normal in other types of writing.

10.6 Punctuating Letters

Letters require very little punctuation, apart from whatever is needed for independent reasons. The address on the envelope looks like this:

Joanna Barker
54 Cedar Grove
Brighton BN1 7ZR

There is no punctuation at all here. Note especially that the number *54* is not followed by a comma. In Britain, it was formerly common practice to put a comma in this position, but such commas are pointless and are no longer usual.

The same goes for the two addresses in the letter itself: your own address (the *return address*), usually placed in the top right-hand corner, and the recipient's address (the *internal address*), usually placed at the left-hand margin, below the return address:

168 Trent Avenue
Newark NG6 7TJ

17 March 1995

Joanna Barker
54 Cedar Grove
Brighton BN1 7ZR

Note the position of the date, and note that the date requires no punctuation.

In British English, the *greeting* is always followed by a comma:

Dear Esther, **or** Dear Mr Jackson,

In American usage, only a personal letter takes a comma here, while a business letter takes a colon:

Dear Esther, **but** (A) Dear Mr. Jackson:

If you are writing to a firm or an institution, and you have no name, you may use the greeting *Dear Sir/Madam*.

The *closing* always takes a comma:

Yours lovingly, **or** Yours faithfully,

Note that only the first word of the closing is capitalized. In British usage, it is traditional to close with *Yours sincerely* when writing to a named person but *Yours faithfully* when using the *Dear Sir/Madam* greeting, but this distinction is anything but crucial. American usage prefers *Yours sincerely* or *Sincerely yours* (A) for all business letters. Things like *Yours exasperatedly* are only appropriate, if at all, in letters to newspapers.

In a personal letter, of course, you can use any closing you like: *Yours lovingly*, *Looking forward to seeing you*, *It's not much fun without you*, or whatever.

Bibliography

Achtert, Walter S. and Joseph Gibaldi. 1985. *The MLA Style Manual*. New York: The Modern Language Association of America.

Carey, G. V. 1958. *Mind the Stop: A Brief Guide to Punctuation*, 2nd edn. London: Penguin.

Pullum, Geoffrey K. 1984. 'Punctuation and human freedom'. *Natural Language and Linguistic Theory* 2: 419–25. Reprinted in Geoffrey K. Pullum, 1991, *The Great Eskimo Vocabulary Hoax and Other Irreverent Essays on the Study of Language*, Chicago: University of Chicago Press, pp. 67–75.

Trask, R. L. 1995. *Language: The Basics*. London: Routledge.

Wells, J. C. 1982. *Accents of English*, 3 vols. Cambridge: Cambridge University Press.

Other Useful Works on Punctuation

Gowers, Sir Ernest. 1962. *The Complete Plain Words*. Harmondsworth: Penguin. Chapter 10: 'Punctuation'.

Jarvie, Gordon. 1992. *Chambers Punctuation Guide*. Edinburgh: Chambers.

Index

READ MORE IN PENGUIN

In every corner of the world, on every subject under the sun, Penguin represents quality and variety – the very best in publishing today.

For complete information about books available from Penguin – including Puffins, Penguin Classics and Arkana – and how to order them, write to us at the appropriate address below. Please note that for copyright reasons the selection of books varies from country to country.

In the United Kingdom: Please write to *Dept. EP, Penguin Books Ltd, Bath Road, Harmondsworth, West Drayton, Middlesex UB7 0DA*

In the United States: Please write to *Consumer Services, Penguin Putnam Inc., 405 Murray Hill Parkway, East Rutherford, New Jersey 07073-2136.* VISA and MasterCard holders call 1-800-631-8571 to order Penguin titles

In Canada: Please write to *Penguin Books Canada Ltd, 10 Alcorn Avenue, Suite 300, Toronto, Ontario M4V 3B2*

In Australia: Please write to *Penguin Books Australia Ltd, 487 Maroondah Highway, Ringwood, Victoria 3134*

In New Zealand: Please write to *Penguin Books (NZ) Ltd, Private Bag 102902, North Shore Mail Centre, Auckland 10*

In India: Please write to *Penguin Books India Pvt Ltd, 11 Community Centre, Panchsheel Park, New Delhi 110017*

In the Netherlands: Please write to *Penguin Books Netherlands bv, Postbus 3507, NL-1001 AH Amsterdam*

In Germany: Please write to *Penguin Books Deutschland GmbH, Metzlerstrasse 26, 60594 Frankfurt am Main*

In Spain: Please write to *Penguin Books S. A., Bravo Murillo 19, 1°B, 28015 Madrid*

In Italy: Please write to *Penguin Italia s.r.l., Via Vittorio Emanuele 45/a, 20094 Corsico, Milano*

In France: Please write to *Penguin France, 12, Rue Prosper Ferradou, 31700 Blagnac*

In Japan: Please write to *Penguin Books Japan Ltd, Iidabashi KM-Bldg, 2-23-9 Koraku, Bunkyo-Ku, Tokyo 112-0004*

In South Africa: Please write to *Penguin Books South Africa (Pty) Ltd, P.O. Box 751093, Gardenview, 2047 Johannesburg*

READ MORE IN PENGUIN

REFERENCE

The Penguin Dictionary of the Third Reich
James Taylor and Warren Shaw

This dictionary provides a full background to the rise of Nazism and the role of Germany in the Second World War. Among the areas covered are the major figures from Nazi politics, arts and industry, the German Resistance, the politics of race and the Nuremberg trials.

The Penguin Biographical Dictionary of Women

This stimulating, informative and entirely new Penguin dictionary of women from all over the world, through the ages, contains over 1,600 clear and concise biographies on major figures from politicians, saints and scientists to poets, film stars and writers.

Roget's Thesaurus of English Words and Phrases
Edited by Betty Kirkpatrick

This new edition of Roget's classic work, now brought up to date for the nineties, will increase anyone's command of the English language. Fully cross-referenced, it includes synonyms of every kind (formal or colloquial, idiomatic and figurative) for almost 900 headings. It is a must for writers and utterly fascinating for any English speaker.

The Penguin Dictionary of International Relations
Graham Evans and Jeffrey Newnham

International relations have undergone a revolution since the end of the Cold War. This new world disorder is fully reflected in this new Penguin dictionary, which is extensively cross-referenced with a select bibliography to aid further study.

The Penguin Guide to Synonyms and Related Words
S. I. Hayakawa

'More helpful than a thesaurus, more humane than a dictionary, the *Guide to Synonyms and Related Words* maps linguistic boundaries with precision, sensitivity to nuance and, on occasion, dry wit' *The Times Literary Supplement*